THE

ROUGH CLOSE

MURDER

THE ROUGH CLOSE MURDER

FOREWORD

I was given this story by Heather Poultney, at a fair in Barlaston, where I had a stall. Heather used to live in the same house where the murder took place, Dale House Farm, Rough Close, Staffordshire. She stated that she and her family had actually heard ghostly phenomena at the house. Heather was also able to give me a layout plan of the house and did say that she thought a family that moved in afterwards, did not stay there long, and she believed they may have moved to France.

So, thank you Heather, for your story. The 1886 story is true, the modern family is not.

I also wish to thank Julie Angel, International Psychic Medium from Malvern in Worcestershire for her grateful help and assistance with reference to the exorcism. Julie is featured in the book, as the medium performing the exorcism. If you are interested, in the paranormal or feel you may need her help, I have given details of Julie's website, at the back of the book.

MARGARET MOXOM

CHAPTER 1

"Put yer back into it, William. Yer nowt but a sissy. Who'd 've thowt I'd breng a sissy into this wereld." This was Thomas Daniel, who was working his farm, Dale House Farm, Rough Close near Longton, Staffordshire. Thomas was a farmer and market gardener (born 1806), with two sons, William and me, John. There were daughters too, and they helped as best they could, milking the cows, collecting the chicken eggs and so on.

"Ah'm doin' may best, pa, but it's darn 'ard wark choppin' thes wooed." William answered.

"Yer nivver listen te may, lad. Ah tells thee 'ow to do sommit, but yer has te do thengs yer own weey. Are yer deef or sommit. Grr, geev it 'ere, ah'll showe yer ageen."

I was there, too, picking up and stacking the chopped logs. I didn't like dad shouting and started to cry. "You can stop yer mithering too, me lad or I'll tan yer 'ide."

Who would have thought I'd bring a sissy into this world. I'm doing my best, pa, but it's darn hard work chipping this wood. You never listen to me, lad. I tell you how to do something, but you have to do things your own way. Are you deaf or something. Grr, give it here, I'll show you again.

I was seven years younger than my brother, and was about 15 at the time.

That was the life on the farm, work, work, work, ploughing, mucking out, feeding the cows and horse, mending fences, going to the market. It was non-stop.

Thomas was always picking on William. I suppose that was what life was like in the late 1850s. He was one of those renowned Victorian fathers. Children should be seen but not heard and, if they were noisy, or didn't obey, they'd get a clout. Still, that's the way life was and the children had to put up with it, and though we didn't have any great love for our father, we at least respected him. He did teach us right from wrong, respect for work, and how to haggle at the market to get the best deals. Of course, he also taught us that, if we did something wrong, we would pay the consequences.

However, William, if he got a hiding, would take it out on me. I couldn't defend myself as I was so much younger. William, would trip me up and shout out to dad that I was a silly little squirt who kept tripping over his own feet. If anything went wrong, he would blame me, He kicked over the milk bucket once or twice and then shout out to dad that I had kicked it over. Of course I'd get a right thrashing from dad. I did try to fight William, but he was so much stronger and taller. He would just hold me at arms' reach, so that I couldn't get to him, laughing all the while, then twist me round and kick me into the mud. I hated him and vowed I would get my own back some day when I was bigger.

Back inside the house was no different, "Won of you childen has made a rate miss in this ketchen, drawers lift open an' oll. Yer'll fayle may belt ef you dosna taydy op."

The 'childen' at the time were my oldest sister, Mary Ann – born 1842, my brother, William, born 1844, then came Sarah (1846), Lydia (1847) Harriett (1849), then me - John Thomas (1851), followed sometime later by little Ann Marie (1858).

So, our mother, Sarah, was just popping them out. Mum was always busy, as you can imagine, feeding babies, cleaning, cooking, although we did have a servant for a while, Sarah Devereux, who was 18 years of age in 1851. Mum was quiet. She didn't have much to say for herself. I think she was belittled by our dad. She saw herself not much more than a servant. What little time she had for herself, in the evening, after the younger children had gone to bed, was spent knitting and sewing.

She wasn't one for reading stories to us, or even making them up, as I don't think her reading was up to much.

One of you children has made a right mess in the kitchen, drawers left open and all. You'll feel my belt if you do no tidy up.

The only time she did come to life a bit was when her family came round and we'd all have a sing song around the old upright piano in the living room. Dad didn't get on with her family – well he didn't get on with many people, so, more often than not, he would take to his bed, saying he had an early start the next morning.

So, I wouldn't say we had a loving childhood, although we did respect our parents.

One day we had to hitch up the horse and cart to go to the market. We loaded up the milk churns and vegetables we had grown, and cheese to sell on. We set up our pitch and I went to have a look round at the other stalls. I came back with a few items I thought we needed. When I returned dad saw red. "You little blayghter. Whut 'ave yer bin op to, spinding may monney and no' aven esking me whut was nayded. 'Ow mooch deed yer paey fur thut robbish? Hasna breens in that thick skull of yurs te know yer've peed mooch more than yer shod've done. Thin yer com back wi' stoff way olriddy has. Whut's wrung wi' yer, lad? Dos I 'ave te wrate everything dine. Go and tek it back. Way dosna nayed it."

You little blighter. What have you been up to, spending my money and not even asking me what was needed? How much did you pay for thus rubbish? Have you no brains in that thick skull of yours to know you have paid much more than you should have done. Then you come back with stuff we already have. What's wrong with you, lad? Do I have to write everything down. Go and take it back. We do not need it.

THE ROUGH CLOSE MURDER

So, I had the humiliating task of asking for my money back. That was a task in its own right as the vendor wasn't having any of it, "I gev yer what yer asked fer, so skiddaddle." I had to stand my ground, "But mister, I gotta get my money back or may dad will leather me." By then I'd managed to collect a crowd around me, all looking on at the commotion I was causing. At last, the vendor relented, egged on by the crowd to show a little compassion.

It was a hard life. I was frightened of my own shadow, no confidence, fearing to do anything in case I got it wrong.

Even when I knew what I was doing, just simple things like picking up the eggs the chickens had laid, I got a rollicking. "Mek sure yer dosna breek any" and, on getting back, "'As yer kynted 'em?" Well, of course I hadn't broken any, and I had counted them. This was something I'd been doing every single day, but I wasn't trusted. It's a horrible feeling not to be trusted to do anything right and it depressed me, so I'd go off to my room and sulk for a bit. Of course, then, I'd get a call, "Weer, the 'ell are yer, theer's melking to be done? You want the poor blayghters te soffer, cos you've got a paddy on? Git dine 'ere, neow!"

I gave you what you asked for, so clear off…

…Make sure you don't break any…. Have you counted them? ….Where the hell are you, there's milking to be done? You want the poor blighters to suffer. Get down here, now.

7

One time I was helping ma get the washing in. It had started to rain so I was in a rush to get the clothes in before they got soaked.

Next minute I felt a right club on my back – hard. It was dad, "Yer coll that fitching washing in. Yer got te fold 'em up afore putting 'em in basket."

"But da, I've got to get the clothes in afore they get soaked. I'll fold them properly when I get indoors."

"So, yer back-chatting yer pa, neow, are yer?" and he hit me again.

I said nothing else. What was the point?

My sister, Sarah, had married back in 1866, as soon as it was legal – I think she couldn't want to get out of the house.

Anyway, in February 1970 William had got married to Annie Barton, and gone to live in Longton. So, at least I was now rid of one pain in my life, and I was the person running the farm with my dad.

You call that fetching the washing in. You've got to fold them before putting them in the basket. ......So you are being disrespectful to your pa, now, are you?

THE ROUGH CLOSE MURDER

My sister, Lydia, had married a Joseph Jukes and gone to live in Tutbury, 54 Monk Street to be precise. Unfortunately, her husband, Joseph died in 1878 and then Lydia herself died the following year. They had had a daughter, also called Lydia. She was only 8 at the time she was left an orphan, so it was decided that little Lydia would come to stay with us, as she had nowhere else to go.

She seemed to get on well with mum, who was teaching her to knit. Mum had left school when she was 12 and, in her last year was teaching the other pupils to knit, something she really enjoyed and, I suppose, little Lydia helped bring back those days in her youth before the humdrum of farm life, bringing babies into the world and a less than caring husband.

Unfortunately, mum died in 1880. That was sad for us but I don't really think she had much to live for. It was yet another death in the family – so much misery.

Soon after, Harriett started looking for a husband and married Henry Tate in October 1881. They went to live in Stone. He was 13 years older than her, but that didn't seem to matter. She wasn't the prettiest lady but she was a young wife, so he was very pleased. We never thought she would get married, and would remain a spinster, but I suppose, when mum died, she didn't see the point of remaining in such a house that had now become so cold. So, at the age of 32 she managed to find herself a nice gentleman to whisk her off.

Of course, later in life, dad got weaker and forgetful. He was now in his 70s and getting quite stooped in his back.

I took my time in finding a wife. I was shy, with no confidence but Susan Downing took me under her wing. I'd got to the grand age of 34, in 1885 when she discovered me. She was five years younger and was everything I needed - I was smitten. She had confidence and style and would put dad in his place, which strangely enough, in his dotage, he accepted. In fact she set about remodelling me, to became a real country gent, wearing the right outfit to meet people, which in itself, with this beautiful lady on my arm, gave me the confidence I had been lacking. She would host soirées and play the piano – not like mum, but more classical, things like Für Elise by Beethoven.

Fur Elise is just a song
A piano tune, Beethoven wrote
It's dedicated to a girl unknown
It's for Elise, a German quote (repeat)

The melody is lyrical
It's beautiful, with ev'ry note
Fur Elise is just a song
A piano tune, Beethoven wrote,
It's dedicated to a girl unknown

THE ROUGH CLOSE MURDER

It's for Elise, a German quote

The melody is lyrical
It's beautiful, with ev'ry note
Fur Elise is just a song,
A piano tune, Beethoven wrote
It's dedicated to a girl unknown
It's for Elise, a German quote.

Susan also started to remodel the farmhouse. She could work her way around dad, with her smiles and charming personality, that he, although begrudgingly, agreed to pay for the changes she had in mind.

Susan had been shocked at the state of the place when she first came to live here. Yes, it was just a basic farmhouse, although quite large. All of the rooms had bare beams for the ceilings. The kitchen and scullery had stone slabs on the floors. The other rooms had bare floorboards. The walls of every room were rough plastered.

Susan wanted to make a comfortable sitting room and dining room, somewhere to relax and where she wouldn't be ashamed to hold her musical soirées.

So she set about getting builders in to put ceilings in the sitting and dining rooms and paper the walls with a flowery flock wallpaper that was in vogue at the time. She also had the rooms carpeted. She had mum's piano in the sitting room, with plenty of chairs and little circular tables with large plants, such as

THE ROUGH CLOSE MURDER

aspidistra, adorning the tables, contained in decorated Staffordshire pots, with pretty lace table cloths. There were also comfy, over-padded settees and armchairs.

Up at the windows were heavy curtains from floor to ceiling with pelmets across the top.

"Now, Mr Daniels and John – you've got these beautiful rooms now, so please may I ask you not to go into either of these rooms with your boots on. We do want to keep the rooms nice, now don't we? So, please can you take off your muddy boots off in the scullery, in future."

Naturally we tried to be observant of her rules but, of course, there were times when we were deep in conversation about sorting something out on the farm, and would walk into the kitchen. A strong scowl in our general direction, then down to our boots, would elicit a sharp detour to the scullery.

To finish off the rooms, Susan had bought loads of pictures to hang all around the walls, and a big ornate mirror over the fireplace. The fireplace surround now had beautifully ornate Minton tiles that really set off the fireplace.

It all looked totally overcrowded to me with all of this strange furniture taking up any little space. You couldn't just walk in and sit down - it now meant a meandering walk avoiding the chairs and tables.

"There", she said, as she got me, on step ladders, to put in hooks to hold some framed photos of ourselves, which we had gone into town especially to get taken. "Now, doesn't that look great? I think Queen Victoria would be proud of what we have achieved. It's the style at present.

Of course, Susan did the same for the dining room, adding a large, highly polished table and matching chairs.

I don't know how or why dad had agreed to all of this and it had definitely made a dent in his bank account – Susan had obviously charmed him, doing anything to make him comfortable and, I suppose, he liked having a pretty, smiling face around. Also he had calmed down a bit over the years and he was getting forgetful. I wasn't really sure if he knew how much Susan had spent. It was he now, who was leaving drawers open. I wouldn't say anything though, just tidy up after him, and make sure he was comfy in his new, padded armchair by the fire in the living room.

Dad did finally put his foot down though, when he finally realised how low his bank account was, and stopped Susan doing any more re-modelling of the house. So, the upstairs rooms were left undecorated.

I'd still get a shout out of him sometimes, "What's oll that racket you're mekking? Can a fella na read his peeper in

What's all that noise your're making? Can't a man read his paper in peace?

14

pace? Ah canna rayd this paper onnyweey, prints too small. Wheer's my magnifying glass?"

I would give him the glass, only for him to leave it on the floor and not put it back in the drawer, where it belonged.

Next minute I got yelled at, "Wheer've yer put glass, yer've tekken it agin. Yer canna layve onything bay." Of course I couldn't tell him it was on the floor, beside him, where he left it as that would be asking for trouble. I'd just pick it up and hand it to him, then wait for him to fall asleep.

I was living with him at the farm, with my lovely wife, Susan, who I had finally managed to pick up enough courage to ask her to marry me and, of course, Lydia, and everything was fine. I don't know why but, more often than not, we just called her 'Jukes' – her surname.

I cannot read this paper anyway, the print is too small. Where's my magnifying glass?

Where have you put the magnifying glass? You can't leave anything alone.

CHAPTER 2

Rough Close was an agricultural village situated midway between Longton and Stone, in North Staffordshire. Our farm house, Dale House, belonging to the family, has several acres of grass land adjoining. It is a substantial, if oddly-constructed three stories erection, standing in its own paddock. Built upon the side of a hill, it faces a charming aspect of undulating though, at this time of the year, a somewhat barren-looking piece of country. The upper portion of it is just discernible from the Stone Road, from which it is approached by a narrow private way, known as Laden Dale Road. Here I, John Daniels, resided, for some time past, with my father, Thomas Daniels, Lydia (Jukes), a niece and lately my wife, Susan Daniels. I was in the habit of attending to the farm, in my father's interests now, as the old gentleman was too worn down with arthritis to look after the homestead himself any longer. This was something that I took on with some relish, feeling that I was now the master of the house.

That was until my brother, William, turned up all of a sudden. He had been living with his family in Normacot. I knew he'd been having financial troubles, mainly because he had taken to drink. Whether this was before the financial troubles or as a result of them, I wouldn't hazard a guess, but I imagine the latter. I wasn't pleased that he had come back to the farm, as we were not particularly close, but I didn't want to rock the boat and welcomed him back. I knew he was strapped for cash and had outstanding bills to be paid, so I paid them for him and bought him a pair of boots, which he was sorely in need of.

He and his wife had obviously been having arguments. I suppose that was on the cards. You can't hope to keep a family and business going if you're wasting all your profits on drink and gambling. I felt sorry for his wife and family.

I asked him when he showed up on the doorstep, "Wheer are Annie en childen?" as I looked around for a carriage but found none.

"Aw, thee've buggered arf. Theer steeying wi' son-in-law, in Neck End (Longton), her en the six childen."

I could smell drink on him as he roughly pushed me aside to stagger past me.

"What's 'appened, William?"

"Nowt te do wi' you."

Where are Annie and the children. Oh, they've gone. They're staying with my son-in-law... my wife end the six children ... Nothing to do with you.

"Well, it is, if yer gonna bay steeying 'ere."

"Aw, git af yer 'igh hoss. Eet's part my 'ise too, so ah'm steeying, whether yer loiks eet or not…. Hey, Susan" he then called out, "Ah nayd sommit to wet may whistle – a whisky mebbee?"

Then he plonked himself, heavily, into the rocking chair in the kitchen as my wife swiftly poured him a whisky.

He then fell asleep. When he woke dad was there over him, with a load of questions. Dad had heard the raised voices, which had woken him. He had been in the living room, sitting in a comfy armchair by the fire and had been dozing.

Confronted by his father, William explained, gruffly, that his business, as a journeyman/gardener, had gone belly up and he couldn't afford to pay the mortgage on the house, so he had to give it up – it was repossessed.

We knew that William's wife had been a widow when he married her. Her first husband, a Mr Burton, met with a sudden, though accidental end, when he fell out of a cart and broke his neck.

…..Well, it is, if you are going to be staying here…… Oh, get off your high horse. It's partly my house too, so I'm staying, whether you like it or not…..I need something to drink, 'm parched – a whisky maybe?

We all knew there were rumours around that William had something to do with the accident, as William had taken a shine to Mr Burton's wife, Annie, but father and I stuck by William. Even though William was questioned by the police, nothing was proved, the report stating that death was due to them both being intoxicated at the time. So it was classed as an unfortunate accident.

"Ah should nivver 'av marrit may Annie." Was all he said.

So, the pleasant calm of the house was no more. We had this drunken slob of my brother, lording it over everyone and, of course, my father, being infirm now, no longer held any fear for him. I didn't want any arguments, so held my tongue.

I should never have married my Annie.

CHAPTER 3

The moving van had worked its way, slowly, up the narrow drive to the house. Dave and Sue, with their two children, Alice and Emily had arrived in their car just a few minutes beforehand and had opened up the main door with the keys that had been placed into Sue's hand by the estate agent, in Longton, just about half an hour before. They were all excited. They'd managed to purchase the house, at auction, for a price they could just about afford. It was a huge house, with large rooms, a living room and dining room downstairs with a kitchen and what was once, they supposed, would have been a scullery. The passageway was wide, with a carved wooden staircase ascending to four bedrooms and a bathroom plus another smaller room. Yes, the house needed a lot doing to it. It just hadn't had much care and attention for many a year. It needed to be brought into up to date. From the money they had saved at the auction, Dave thought they had a bit spare to get workmen in to do the technical stuff, while he and Sue, with the help of a few friends, would set about decorating it. The front door had creaked as Sue turned the key to open it. "Oh, that needs a bit of oiling for a start," Dave stated.

"More than that, Dave, look, the varnish is peeling off and I'm not sure if the wood is actually rotten underneath."

THE ROUGH CLOSE MURDER

Dave, in his up frame of mind thought he'd try to raise Sue's mood, "Is there anything that runs around a garden without actually moving?"

"I don't know, Dave."

"A fence."

"OK, we know you're a born comedian." Sue replied.

Looking at all the boxes being unloaded, Dave quipped, "The heart is where the home is, even if you can't remember which box you packed it in."

"That's not funny." Sue said. You know we labelled each box, but that's before we had actually sorted out what we were going to use the rooms for. This is a nightmare."

After tea, we decided to have a walk around the house together, to see what needed doing. The house had been empty for some time and was in a poor state of repair, as we knew when we had the one and only opportunity to see it before the auction, but we'd fallen in love with it at first sight.

GROUND FLOOR			
Kitchen	Pantry	Back Door	Covered walkway
	Passage	Back Stairs ‖‖‖	Scullery
Sitting Room	Hall Front Door	Cellar Steps ‖‖‖	Living Room (Cellar under living room)

FIRST FLOOR (attic rooms over two front bedrooms)			
Bedroom	Bathroom	Toilet	Bedroom
	Landing Step down	Back stairs ‖‖‖	
Bedroom	Landing	Stairs to attic| ‖‖	Bedroom
	Dressing room		

THE ROUGH CLOSE MURDER

Dave went to inspect, "You might be right, we only got a quick viewing before the auction and there's loads to be done from what I can remember."

"Anyway, the removal men are waiting to get in. We'll just have to tell them to put our stuff where they can for now. All the bedroom furniture is labelled for upstairs. Everything else is labelled for whatever room they are going to downstairs. We'll have to sort everything out eventually."

Dave said, "It's a shame we couldn't just put our stuff in store for the time being until we got the place fixed up, but it would have been far too expensive."

"Yes, it's also a shame we had to get out of our old house there and then, but we had to sell up to get this house and, as you know, the new people are moving into our old house today."

Alice and Emily, in the meantime, were skipping around quite noisily, nosing into every room. You could hear their giggles as they opened this and that door and every cupboard they could find. During the day I think they started to play hide and seek. The place was so large, it was easy to do so, especially as it had a cellar under the living room and an attic over the two front bedrooms, with stairs going up and down to both.

At one point, Emily, being only 5 years old, came running to us in tears, "I can't find Alice."

Dave came to the rescue, shouting out in the downstairs hall, "Come on Alice, you know not to taunt Emily. You are three years older and should know better. Anyway, your mum is preparing something to eat, so you'd better come down, otherwise you're going to miss out on the treats. We're in the kitchen."

There wasn't actually a table to put anything on in the kitchen as everything was packed up in boxes, with bubble wrap around furniture, but Dave managed to free some of the dining room chairs and a set of occasional tables. I'd bought some pre-packed sandwiches and juice for the girls. We'd have to make do with a large bottle of cola shared between us until we could find the electric kettle and tea bags or coffee, then maybe a bottle of wine, when we'd found the glasses that is, for later, when the girls were in bed.

At that moment, we heard scurrying feet and Alice appeared at the kitchen door. "I won, I won, Emily. You couldn't find me." To which Emily stuck out her tongue then said, "But I'm gonna get to eat first, so there!" and she picked up a big gooey cake, which she began to devour.

CHAPTER 4

The girls then went off to play while we did the grand tour and tried to formulate some ideas on how we wanted the place to look.

The kitchen itself had old hand-made cupboards. They must have been at least 60 years old, probably a lot more, and dirty. The floor was stone slabs. There was an old Raeburn but we had been told that it was defunct, so couldn't be used.

"I want to keep the place still like a farmhouse, but modernise it, Dave. We'll need new cupboards, but farmhouse style, and I would like an island in the centre, with seating where we can have breakfast."

"What do you think of the floor? It would be a right job hauling up those stones. I think we should keep them."

"You're probably right, Dave, but we need a new Raeburn and…" going into the hall, passed what used to be the pantry, passed the wide carved oak staircase leading upstairs, then on into the scullery, and looking around "….probably a new boiler. This could be the laundry room."

"A friend of mine used to install kitchen work surfaces."

25

"Oh, that's good to know, can we contact him?"

"No, he was arrested for counter fitting..... I'm sorry Sue, caught you out with that one."

"You're a silly bugger sometimes, Dave." and she gave him a little punch to the ribs for winding her up.

"Ooh that hurt." Dave pretended to buckle over in pain.

"No it didn't you big softy."

"Anyway, enough of that. Just remember, Sue, the well isn't full to overflowing. We'll have to just do the things that are absolutely vital, then do bits and pieces as I get a bit more money."

"I know it will take a time, Dave, but I'm just so excited with what could be done." And we gave each other a hug. "Yes, we'll just have to make do and mend for the time being, a bit of paint and paper, such as the ceiling in the kitchen." Then looking up, "Just look at those lovely old beams."

"Yes, a bit of a rub down of the beams, varnish them, and paint the ceiling white."

Going on through the scullery, into another room I said, "This is a huge room," and looking up, "and beautiful old beams again." The fireplace was massive, going back some distance, and a long mantelpiece, quite high, stretching almost the width of the chimney breast. "I suppose this could be the living room – and look, an

26

upright piano has been left." Sue played a few notes. "It needs tuning, but I think we'll keep it. Look, there's an old armchair as well. It's seen better days, but I could recover it. It looks sturdy enough. I see this as a sitting room, loads of comfy seats and armchairs, with a large screen TV. Then again, if the fire were to be blocked off, then a TV could go there on a stand. A huge mirror over the mantelpiece would set the place off. What do you think, Dave?"

"Oh, sounds good, but we'll need some heating if you're going to get rid of the fireplace. Underfloor heating would do the job."

"Yes, if we build a sort of boxed-in alcove in the centre of this huge fireplace, about the size of say, a gas fire, but with some depth to it, we could have a feature there - a piece of artwork or flower display in that boxed-in area."

We carried on through another door leading back to the long hall, but we were now by the front door, and there were yet more stairs, these ones going down. "Oh, a cellar too – imagine us, with guests, and, putting on a posh accent said, "Dave, I believe our guests need a top up, can you just go to the wine cellar for more wine please."

"Oh course, madam." Dave replied, and we both laughed.

We crossed the hall into another large room. "Oh, this is ridiculous, Dave. Does this place never end?" This room also had beams and a huge fireplace with Milton tiles as decoration.

"That's beautiful. Shame we can't light coal fires anymore." Dave added. We'll have to replace that, get it blocked up, put a modern glass-fronted gas fire in its place. But, as you said, we'll have to get one that will enable us to keep the tiles."

"Yes, this could, I suppose, be the dining room - it's right next to the kitchen, so would save crossing the hall, and the food getting cold.

We went back out into the hallway and along to the back door, then up the stairs, where we found not just the four bedrooms but another smaller room. "I've no idea what we could use this for. Maybe a playroom for the two girls, or even a dressing room, to keep all of our winter gear. I don't know, we'll have to think about that. I feel we should be in a Bet Davis film, or one of those black and white 19th century period films, where everyone is rich, bedecked with jewels, and they have a dressing room with a maid, say, helping Bet Davis with her hair. I need a maid, Dave!"

"You need a maid as much as I need a valet, girl. Yes, come to think of it, a valet would suit me down to the ground." And he strutted around, brushing off his t-shirt and jeans, as though he were wearing a Saville Row suit.

"Yes, sir. By all means, sir. Is there anything else I can get you sir?"

We laughed again. "How did we ever manage to get this place so cheaply?"

THE ROUGH CLOSE MURDER

"Well, we were really lucky, there was no-one else bidding for it, not even a building company, and you know what they're like, see this, turn it into flats, and chink, chink, the money would come rolling in."

So, we finished our tour of upstairs, noting the separate toilet and bathroom. The bathroom had one of those old roll-top baths, away from the wall. "This is great, they're really coming into fashion again, and it's not really in bad nick, even though it's so old."

There were stairs opposite leading up to the attic, but we would keep that for another day. Time to do some unpacking now – especially the girls' beds, as time was getting on.

The girls' were worn out with running up and down different staircases, screaming and shouting. There were no curtains up at the windows but I knew as soon as their heads hit the pillows they would be sound asleep.

Dave still managed to find a book and read them a story, but he was only one chapter in when their eyes had closed and they were in the land of nod.

We found the wine and two glasses and cuddled up on the sofa, even though it was still wrapped in bubble-wrap and cardboard. We'd just got the mattress for our bed unwrapped. We'd sleep on the mattress on the floor just for this night and dream of our wonderful house.

In bed, Dave remembered, "Oh, of course, there used to be more land attached, as it had been a working farm at one time, but that land has been sold off."

"And good job too, I can't see me trying to mow a field with my little hover-mower." We laughed at the thought of me, sweating cobs, taking the hover-mower through the divots and tuffs of wild grass.

"Then again, you could have made a 9-hole golf course, or we could have kept ponies for the girls."

"Too bad, we haven't got the land, so good night, sleep tight and sweet dreams, then he kissed me and I fell asleep in his arms.

CHAPTER 5

Dave worked in Longton, for himself, as a supplier of farming equipment and tools. He had a small team of workers and a factory, where tools were repaired.

I worked as a supply teacher – 8-11 year olds.

We found a good school for the girls and they soon started to make friends.

I was always busy as, if I wasn't needed at a school, I would be helping Dave with his business, keeping the books up to date and taking orders, as well as the usual cooking meals, washing and looking after the girls when they came back from school. If the phone in Dave's office wasn't answered after a couple of rings, it would divert to my mobile, so I could take the customers' details and requests. So, I didn't really have much time to work on the house, except some evenings and weekends, but it was coming along.

I had arranged for kitchen builders to remove the old kitchen and put in new units, so that was something at least. There was a brilliant place near Festival Park, and we took advantage of their summer half-price sale. Of course, the walls needed plastering and I had painted them, once the plaster was dry. It wasn't much fun, being up a ladder, then the phone would ring, so I'd have to scurry down and take details, for say a plough that needed repairing. Then I would have to put this order on the computer. Then, of course, I would have to wipe the phone over with a wet wipe, as I would more than likely have paint on my hands. Luckily, the paint I was using was water- and not oil-based.

The girls would be coming in for their tea soon, so I knew I'd have to pack up everything and start preparing something.

It was just then I heard footsteps upstairs, running across the bedroom above the kitchen. I called out, "Girls, have you come in the front door? Are you up there? You could at least have come and said you were back from school? Now that's not polite is it? Come down now."

There was no answer, and the running footsteps had stopped. I called out again, "Girls, are you up there?" No answer. So I went through to the hall and up the stairs. There was no-one there, anywhere. I checked all of the rooms.

"Very strange," I said to myself. "Maybe I imagined it, or a bird had got in, or something."

I told Dave about it when he got home. "Oh, these old houses, you know what they're like, they creak and crack. It will be the floorboards drying out in the heat. You know we haven't got any floor board covering in those rooms upstairs yet. Nothing to worry about, silly sausage."

THE ROUGH CLOSE MURDER

So I put it out of my mind.

CHAPTER 6

"Jukes, your uncle William will need a bed making up for him." This was Susan giving instructions to Beatrice, the orphaned niece, who was now living with them.

"The bedroom above the kitchen is not in use, so make up the bed there, if you please."

John was outside in the fields with his father.

Jukes scurried off and we could hear her upstairs, after getting sheets from the airing cupboard in the hallway upstairs, running around the bed from side to side, getting the bed in order.

"You trayte that pooer lass just loik a scullery maid, missie 'igh en maighty."

"William, that is totally out of order. I am not her governor. She's helping me with anything I need help with, and she's much appreciated. I couldn't do without her."

You treat that poor lass just like a scullery maid. Missie high and mighty

THE ROUGH CLOSE MURDER

"Yer, ah bet yer gets her doing onything yer dosna fancy doing yersen, while you sit, at your leisure, Ah bets shay does all washing en ironing as well as cleaning en mekking up fires."

"Jukes has been really helpful but she is not my maid and is part of our family and is treated as such. And, must I say, if I do sit down, it is because I am working, knitting and mending clothes."

"Yer'd 'av 'er doing that too, if shay could, ah bet."

"William, you are being quite out of order, if I may say so, and I do not care for your attitude. If you must know, Jukes is quite the good knitter, your mother taught her."

"Who are you to tell may ah'm ite of order. Yer nowt 'ere but a neuwcomer, so ah'd keep yer mouth shut eef thah knows what sade yer bread's buttered!"

"I am your brother's legal wife, and this is my home too. You are the interloper here, William, and you know it. You had your own home and you have your own family."

Yes, I bet you get her doing anything you don't fancy doing yourself..... and making up the fires.... You would have her doing that too.... Who are you to tell me I am out of order. You're nothing but a newcomer, so I'd keep your mouth shut if you knows what side your bread is buttered.

35

"Ay, that's roit, but this is may family 'ome, and eet's moin too, so donna fergit it.At that, William got up and lurched into another room.

He soon came back. "Whut's bin 'appening 'ere. Yer've gone en changed ivverthing. Miss 'igh en mighty 'as put 'er stamp ont place. Eet looks loik an 'ore ise wi' oll those foncy beets en bobs en plants. But, ah mun seey, eet suits you. An 'ore in an 'ore ise!"

At that point, Susan ran out of the room. She burst into tears. She heard William shouting out behind her, "No good running to that weakling brother o' moin. Eet's your word agin moin."

John wasn't there to defend her and she knew that William would just deny saying anything so awful to her. She'd just have to grin and bear it, put a brave face on.

Yes, that's right, but this is my family home, and it's mine too, so don't forget it.

What's been happening here? You've gone and changed everything. It looks like a whore house, with all those fancy bits and bobs and plants. But I must say it suits you. A whore in a whore house.

…brother of mine. It's your word against mine.

CHAPTER 7

Things didn't get any better. Whenever John and the father were out of the house and Jukes was busy elsewhere, William would turn on Susan.

"I 'ear yer plonking on that old Joanna – think yer con pleey, eh. Well, eet sineds loik a cat up an old alley. Ah dosna know whut yer so called guests thenk on it. 'Spose theer just baying polite."

Susan was biting her tongue, trying not to get roused by him. "Whatever you say, William, you have a right to your own opinion."

William had the wherewithal, even in his drunken state, not to say anything to any guests they might have. He didn't want them turning on him. He'd just go into another room, until any guests had left, and drink his whisky, then fall asleep.

I here you've been plonking on that old piano – think you can play, eh. Well, it sounds like…I don't know what your so-called guests think of it. I suppose they are just being polite

Yes, he knew he was being obnoxious. He knew he drank too much, but sometimes he just couldn't help himself and he'd pick on the person in the house who couldn't or wouldn't defend herself, and that was Susan. He didn't like her anyway, stuck up witch. It was a bit of a game to him. He loved to see her squirm and, if she tried to come back with any comments, he knew he could just up the ante and bombard her with more outrageous remarks. Yes, Susan would ignore him, but that was all part of the entertainment, as he saw it. It just meant he had to think of something else to rile her.

He wouldn't pick on Jukes, as she was family and only young – there was no sport in that.

Everything had gone wrong for him. He'd lost his house, his business and his family were estranged from him. He tried to tell himself it was not all his fault, In his mind everyone and everything were against him.

Still, he made himself useful, when he wasn't so drunk, and helped on the farm. He couldn't have his father and brother pick on him and tell him he was a waster. In his mind, given a bit of time, he could get back on his feet, build a business up again and get his family back. All he needed was time…. and some money.

He had tried to get round his father to get some money from him, but, even though his father was in his dotage, he kept a tight hold of the purse strings. He'd say,

THE ROUGH CLOSE MURDER

"There's no money here. You'll have to earn it and, until I can see you're pulling your weight, there'll be nothing coming from me."

Of course, this denial backfired onto Susan. "Eet's all your fote theer's nay monney int 'ise – yer've gone en spint it oll on yer faneries en frills. Yer've gone en spent may enayritance, you owd weetch. Eet's 'cos of you, ah cosna git back on may fayte."

Then he'd say, "Yes, yer owd and ugly – ah dosna know whut may brother seeys in yer. En yer gitting fot!"

Susan had to say something to that, "If you must know, William, John and I are awaiting a happy event – if that's what you call getting fat! John loves me and we are happily married, more than you are anymore."

"Greee, when's the brat due?"

"In March. So that's why I ask Jukes to do all the heavy work about the place. She's been a Godsend."

It's all your fault there's no money in the house. You've gone and spent it all.- spent my inheritance, you old witch. It's because of you, I cannot get back on my feet. You're old and ugly – I don't know what my brother sees in you. And you're getting fat.

"Skivvy, more loik it. In owr family, ma worked til shay dropped, none of this," and mimicking her, "I'm too delicate to do any hard work… malarkey."

"Yes, and look where it got her. In an early grave."

"You lave may mother ite o' this."

"You started it, William."

Skivvy, more like it. In our family….You leave my mother out of this.

CHAPTER 8

The work on the house was coming on bit by bit. The underfloor heating had gone down in the living room, the fire place had been boarded up and there was a large TV in situ on a low cabinet, but not in front of the defunct fireplace but in a family and guest- seating space. We had raided the antique and second-hand shops in the area and managed to get corner sofas. I had managed to find some appropriate material to re-cover the old armchair that had been left there. The sitting room looked really cosy, with occasional tables and leafy plants, with book cases in the alcoves plus Sue had placed a small statue in the fireplace, with plants at the back. Vertical blinds were up at the windows plus heavy patterned curtains to match wallpaper over the chimney breast. All the walls and woodwork had been painted throughout the house, in a beige colour, which was the in-colour at the present time.

There was still plenty to do and the upstairs had really not been touched, apart from curtains.

Anyway, I had some unexpected news for Dave, which took me by surprise as well. I was pregnant! The baby was due in March. Luckily, all the work up ladders was finished, for the time being anyway. Maybe next year I'd start on upstairs, apart from painting a room for the new baby.

"What about the dressing room upstairs, Dave? Do you think that would make a suitable nursery?"

"Yes, why not, it is right next to our bedroom so, if you hear the baby crying, you can get up and tend to it."

"I'm having none of that, Dave. If WE hear the baby crying, you or I can get up and tend to it."

"Oh, you are a dolt, of course, I meant that. I was only joking, just to wind you up."

"Well, I don't need any winding up, thank you."

……

I still kept on hearing the noises upstairs but I didn't give it much further thought, that's until I heard what couldn't be anything else except someone opening and shutting the drawers on a cupboard in the upstairs hallway. The hairs went up on the back of my head. There was no-one else in the building, no workmen, Dave was at his works and the children were at school.

I ran up the stairs as fast as I could – I wasn't heavily pregnant so could still do so, but there was no-one there. I looked in the cupboard and everything seemed to be straight and ordered as I had left it – the sheets, towels and extra bedding were kept there.

I looked in all the rooms again. No-one and nothing out of place.

THE ROUGH CLOSE MURDER

When Dave got back that evening, I told him how scared I felt.

"You do believe me, don't you?"

"Yes, of course, darling. It's just a shame I wasn't here to witness it."

"There, you don't believe me!"

"Oh, what do you want me to say? Whatever I say will be wrong."

"Is there some sort of camera we can get installed, that will play when someone or something goes past?"

"Yes, of course, but I still think it might just be your hormones and you are over-reacting. It's probably your mothering instinct for protection of you and your unborn child just kicking in."

"OUR unborn child, you uncaring sonofabitch."

"No need for that, lovely, it was just a slip of the tongue. I'm sorry – our unborn child. Please forgive me."

"You do want this child, don't you? I know it is unexpected, but…"

"Of course I do, and you never know, it could be a boy this time. So, I could have someone to play football with."

"Oh, silly, give him a chance to be born first, let alone grow enough to play football."

"So, I'm forgiven?"

"Yes,..... just this time though." And they embraced. Though, Sue wasn't really happy. Dave had been so excited finding out about Emily and Alice, treating her like a queen, waiting on her every whim. She was getting the distinct impression that Dave wasn't all that keen on this pregnancy. He'd never said 'your' baby before, instead our 'our'.

"Still," Sue continued, coming out of the seeming tactlessness of her husband, that was making her slightly unhappy. "I don't think it's my hormones. It's something else, and it's frightening."

"Ok. I'll get a camera set up. You never know, in an old house like this, we could have ghosts. Whooo!"

CHAPTER 9

To cheer herself up and to escape the horror of William's tirades. Susan decided to hold one of her soirées. At least she knew that William would slope off to another room.

She would invite the neighbours, as usual, including Mrs Emma Latham and her husband Mr Henry Latham, and George Gould of Leydon Dale. She also invited John Duval who, although the postman, was very fond of classical music. Jukes would accompany Susan on the recorder.

The evening went well, with Mrs Latham, adding a singing accompaniment. John Duval also had a quite good tenor voice, to add to the evening's entertainment.

Susan started the evening with The Waves of the Danube, a waltz composed by Iosif Ivanocivi in 1880. It was very reminiscent of the music of Johann Strauss. (known later as The Anniversary Song).

This was followed by an excerpt from the opera Carmen, by Georges Bizet, Habanera, sung by Mrs Latham:

"L'amour est enfent de bohême

Il n'a jamais, jamais connu de loi
Si tu ne m'aimes pas, je t'aime
Si je t'aimes prends garde à toi.
Prends garde à toi.
Si tu ne m'aimes pas, je t'aime
Prends garde à toi.
Mais si je t'aime, si je t'aime
Prends garde à toi."

Translation:

(Love is the child of Bohemia,
It has never, never known the law,
If you don't love me, I love you
If I love you, keep guard of you
If you don't love me,
If you don't love me, I love you
But, if I love you, if I love you,
keep guard of you)

Then John Duval added his tenor tones to a rendition of Toreador;

Of course, Gilbert and Sullivan were very popular at the time so, an evening would not be the same without a song from The Pirates of Penzance, which was so fast it would leave John Duval fighting for breathe and poor Susan's fingers flying on the piano, trying to keep up:

"I am the very model of a modern major general
I've information vegetable, animal and mineral

THE ROUGH CLOSE MURDER

I know the kings of England, and I quote the fights historical
From Marathon to Waterloo, in order categorical;
I'm very well acquainted, too, with matters mathematical
I understand equations, both the simple and quadrilatical
About binomial thorium I'm teeming with a lot o' news
With many cheerful facts about the square of the hypotenuse."

This was followed by the popular and uplifting Funiculi, Funicula, where everyone joined in the chorus –

"Some think the world is made for fun and frolic,
and so do I, and so do I.
Some think it well to be all melancholic,
to pine and sigh, to pine and sigh.
But I love to spend my time in singing,
some joyous song, some joyous song.
To set the air with music bravely ringing,
is far from wrong, is far from wrong.
Listen, listen, music sounds a-far.
Listen, listen, with a happy heart.
Funiculi, Funicula, Funiculi, Funicula.
Joy is everywhere, Funiculi, Funicula."

To calm down the evening, they all sang the Skye Boat Song, lyrics by Sir Harold Edwin Boulton

"Speed bonnie boat, like a bird on the wing
Onward the sailors cry.

Carry the lad that's born to be king
Over the sea to Skye….."

The evening finished with Susan, on the piano, playing
The Londonderry Air.

CHAPTER 10

"This cupboard by the back door, Dave, that I think used to be the pantry."

"Oh, I can see you've got that look again. You've got something else for me to do. Come on then, let me have it. What have you got in mind?"

"Well, we don't need a pantry, as we've got all the cupboard space we need in the kitchen now, plus the fridge and freezer. I was just thinking that possibly it could be used as a coat and boot room. We need somewhere to hang our coats. We could also store holiday luggage ready for when we can afford to go on a holiday again."

"So, it's not just a room you want, you want to have a holiday as well?"

"Oh, don't read more into what I'm saying, Dave. One day we'll have a holiday again but, I was looking in that cupboard and there doesn't seem to be a light, not one that works anyway. Maybe the wiring's broken."

Dave went to check it over. "Hmm. We had the new consumer unit put in but the electrician doesn't seem to have checked the cabling in this cupboard. It seems such a small thing to do, just check the wiring is connected first of all, before we pay out for the electrician again. I can do that."

So Dave went to get his ladder and tools. "I'll just make sure the electricity is off first. The girls are watching TV in the lounge, so I'll keep that switch on. I can't see the cable running all the way from the living room to this cupboard. It must run from the scullery or kitchen or the hallway. I'll turn those off."

So, Dave flicked the switches and set to work to undo the cover plate for the light switch. I was looking at the consumer box, just looking at the labels the electrician had put against the switches for each room. That's when I noticed that the hall switch was half way up, not off. Dave must have just flicked it and it flicked back and hadn't noticed. It was high up and I was trying to reach it to turn it off when I heard a bang, a terrific scream from Dave and a loud crash.

"Oh God", and I ran to see if he was alright. Dave was lying at the bottom of the stairs. He looked unconscious. "Dave, Dave, are you ok," I yelled, while checking his pulse. He looked as white as a sheet and his hair was standing on end. He was alive. I could see his eyelids fluttering. "Dave, talk to me. I'll call an ambulance."

The girls had come running. "All the lights and the TV have gone off." Emily said, before looking down at her father. Seeing him prone on the floor she started to cry then Alice started too. I had to ignore them and ran for my phone, returning to Dave as I was dialling. By this time, Dave was coming to and, in a very shaky voice said,

50

"I'm alright, honey. Gawd that hurt." then started rubbing the back of his head. "I think you must have been thrown backwards into the newel post and bashed your head."

"I feel wretched"

"I've called for an ambulance. The hospital needs to check you over. I was just about to call out to warn you that the hallway switch hadn't gone fully off, it must have sprung back. I couldn't reach it to turn it off."

Dave tried to sit up. He was breathless "I feel like I'm in a fog. I can't see you clearly. My chest hurts." He was trying to catch his breath, with his mouth open, holding a hand against his chest. I thought he was going to have a heart attack. "Lie down Dave."

"I feel sick." He was making a rasping sound and his voice was deeper and rougher.

"Get a bowl girls" I shouted and went to get a coat to cover him up and a cushion for his head. I came back and held his hand, "Stay with us Dave, the ambulance will be here soon. "

The ambulance arrived and Dave was taken to hospital. We couldn't all get in the ambulance so I following behind in the car with the girls.

Luckily Dave hadn't received any electrical burns but was kept in for observation, fearing a concussion.

When we were all home again, Dave still didn't seem to be his normal self. His voice was huskier and deeper. He didn't seem to be totally aware of his surroundings and would spend most of his time seated, in an armchair or in the kitchen, in a rocking chair that had been left there by the previous owners.

There was something else though. I would see him mumbling, sort of talking to himself, even what looked like having arguments with himself. He wouldn't talk to me about it.

After a few days, Dave said, "I need to get out of here. I don't feel right, but I'm going to work." There was no way I could stop him and I felt that he needed to get out and have his mind on something else other than the accident, so I let him go.

And so it continued. Work didn't seem to help. He would come back through that door in the same state that he left. We didn't really talk much anymore, only about work. Some days were better than others though, so he wasn't constantly in the deep, silent mood he exhibited. He did enjoy interacting with the girls. One thing that really upset me was that he didn't ask about the baby, although I would tell him if I felt the baby move. I really wanted to just shout at him sometimes, just to get a response, but I didn't. I told myself I'd just have to wait and be calm and things would improve. If he wouldn't say much to me, I would still keep up a one-sided conversation, telling him everything the girls were getting up to in school, even attempting a joke or two but, on bad days, I didn't get much of a response. He could laugh with the girls, but

THE ROUGH CLOSE MURDER

was quite cold towards me. Intimacy had gone out of the window.

CHAPTER 11

I was busy early one evening, working on Dave's accounts. I was in the dining room, using the big dining table to keep the invoices in order.

The rest of the family were in the living room, playing board games waiting for their favourite tv programme to come on, it was a cartoon film. They'd just have about enough time to see the film, before Dave packed the two girls off to bed.

I was trying to concentrate but, somehow or other, tunes kept popping into my head, old tunes that I hadn't heard of in a while.

I found myself singing along to a few. They were quite jolly, "Funiculi, funicula, la la la la la, funiculi, funicula.

Then there were the strains of the Skye Boat Song going through my head. I loved that song and remembered singing it at school. The story of Bonnie Prince Charlie finding refuge on the Isle of Skye, following his defeat at the Battle of Culloden. He disguised himself as a woman, with the aid of Flora Macdonald, to avoid capture by the English Soldiers.

THE ROUGH CLOSE MURDER

It's then that I realised that the songs were not in my head. I could hear them clearly, as coming through the walls from the direction of the living room.

"Maybe they've put the TV on in there, onto a music programme, Sky Arts maybe." I said to myself.

Being interested I got up to investigate but, entering the living room, there was no TV on and the girls were playing a board game. They definitely weren't singing.

It must have been one of those rare friendly days. Dave was in a good mood with the girls, and didn't seem troubled, "Hey girls, what's the most fruitful subject at school?"

"Oh, oh, I know that, daddy" Emily shouted out, "It's history, because it's full of dates."

"Very good Emily."

I interrupted, "You haven't been playing any music have you, Dave?"

"No, Sue. Just been playing reasonably quietly. Emily has been cheating and Alice got a bit upset, so I had to quieten them down, as I knew you were concentrating next door, but no, no music."

"That's very strange. I can still hear it. Can't you hear anything? Yes, there are people singing…. It's Danny Boy, my mum's favourite – words put to The Londonderry Air."

55

Alice commented, "Oh, you've got yourself too tired, concentrating too much." She sounded quite grown up – must have picked that up from me, I thought. "Come and have a sit down and watch the film with us. It's coming on any minute now." she beckoned.

"No, listen. Girls be quiet! Hush."

"Come to think of it, Susan, yes, I can vaguely hear something. It's coming in the direction of the piano." It was strange he called me Susan, as he'd always just called me Sue, but I didn't think much of it. Just one of those things.

They both walked up to the piano and Dave quietly repeated the words he could hear. "But when ye come, and all the flowers are dying, if I am dead, as dead I well may be, you'll come and find the place where I am lying, and kneel and say an Ave there for me."

"Yes, that's it exactly. It's exactly what I hear. I didn't know there was a second verse. I didn't know those words."

"Oh, then we've definitely got ghosts. No good having the camera upstairs then, as the camera won't pick up ghosts. Oh well, so we've got memories coming through of the past. There's nothing wrong with that. They're not causing any mischief, just pleasant music. Let's just let them be."

"OK, if you say so, Dave. But it's weird, very weird."

THE ROUGH CLOSE MURDER

"Let's have a drink. I've really for a taste for a whisky. I can taste it in my mouth."

"You don't drink whisky, Dave. I've only ever known you to drink wine or the occasional beer. Besides that, we haven't got whisky in the house and you know we can't have a drink until the children have gone to bed." "Spoilsport. Always trying to make out I'm in the wrong all the time." Dave suddenly said, quite malevolently.

"Dave, what's got into you all of a sudden? I really haven't said anything out of line. If you're so desperate for a whisky, go down the pub and I'll look after the girls, but don't come back roaring drunk, otherwise I'll make you sleep in the spare room."

"There you go again, having a go at me before I've even done anything. I just said I fancied a whisky, not that I was going to get drunk."

"Oh, Dave. I'm not having a go at you, just don't know what's got into you lately."

"There, my fault again."

"Oh, it's no good talking to you when you're in this mood. I'm going back to the books. If you go out, let me know…. Oh, and by the way, whoever, keeps moving that armchair in the living room to in front of the blocked up fire place, please put it back again. It's not meant to be there and why put it in front of a defunct chimney breast, I've no idea. Also, I keep finding newspapers on the floor by that armchair and, for some unknown reason, the magnifying glass I use to read the small print in contracts, is on the floor there too. That belongs in the sideboard drawer, and the newspapers should be in the TV magazine rack, so clear up after you….. please."

I then stormed out, not waiting for an answer.

CHAPTER 12

It was 15 January, 1886 and we had a visitor. He wasn't bringing good news. It was William and John's brother-in-law, John Bennett, married to their sister. Sarah. They were living in Normacot, with their children. They had four children, Sarah Elizabeth, John Thomas, Joseph Edwin and Amelia.

"Sarah's sickly. Shay's bad. Ah've called doctor, but 'e canna do onything fur 'er. Ah'm 'ere to seey, shay's na got long to live."

We all gathered round to hear his bad tidings and to offer what help we could. William said, "Of course, the childen can come ov'r 'ere, steey wi' us. Way'll put 'em up."

"I'll come back with you John" Susan offered, "Not that I can be much use, but I'll try to make Sarah's last days more comfortable."

The offer was taken up.

I'm here to say, she's not got long to live.
Of course the children can come over here, stay with us. We'll put them up.

Sarah died on 27th January 1886. The funeral was arranged for 3rd February. John Daniel said he would make arrangements for the funeral but left it in his wife's capable hands, believing her to have good taste. However, William expressed his views that he was not happy with these arrangements, saying that his brother, John, had cut corners to save money. "Shay's owr sister, John, way donna 'ave te spare monney fer owr sister! Way should gee 'er a roit gooed send-af."

At the funeral, everyone was, naturally, dreadfully sorry, and trying to comfort John Bennett, but suddenly, and I don't know why, he became enraged. There were a lot of raised voices. William then said to his brother, "Ah telt yer yer shod've spent mer monney ont funeral. Yer con seey e's no 'appy." It's your bloody wife, John. Yer've ge'en 'er reins ont monney en shay's tightened 'em. Yer shod've telt 'er to kayp 'er bloody nose ite."

John Bennett was pushing people away from him then, just as suddenly, started physically pounding at his two brothers-in-law, William and John. Of course, it was one against two and William and John defended themselves, giving him a right thrashing. John was, obviously trying to defend his wife's honour, although not knowing what

---

She's our sister.. we don't have to save on money for our sister! We should give her a right good send-off....I told you you should've spent more money on the funeral. You can see he's not happy...You've given her the reins on the money, and she's tightened them. You should have told her to keep her bloody nose out.

Susan may or may not have said. John Bennett ended up on a heap on the ground, holding his head in his hands, nursing his wounds.

Everyone else was so taken aback so much that the police were called.

William and John actually took out a summons against John Bennett for starting the fight. The case was mentioned at the Longton Borough Court the next Monday, where it was ascertained that money matters were believed to be at the bottom of the dispute. The Court decided to hold the case over, as it was deemed to be a family dispute and it was hoped that the three parties could come to some agreement. However, instead of discussing the matter, John Bennett took out a cross-summonses against William and John Daniel. This was to be heard the following Monday.

CHAPTER 13

"Girls, have you moved that little statue in the fireplace? I found it tucked behind one of the settees." Sue asked. "I won't be annoyed with you, I'd just like to know. It's just that I keep finding things moved, just like the armchair being moved to the chimney breast area and it's puzzling. Your dad says he's not moved it."

"No, mum. The armchair is much too heavy for us to move anyway. Look." and Alice tried to shift it, but couldn't.

"Oh well, another thing to put down to the ghosts."

"Don't go away, mum. We want to talk." Alice said.

"Yes, sweetie, I'm always here. Is something bothering you."

"Well, we're worried about dad. Is he not well? It's just that he's hardly here and, when he is, he falls asleep in an armchair. He doesn't play with us anymore. And, well, I don't like to say this but there's a strange smell about him."

"Oh." Sue took a bit of time answering as she wasn't sure what to say. "Yes, my sweets, daddy isn't too well at the moment. He's getting very tired as he's working too hard at the shop. Just let him sleep. Play in another room. As for the strange smell, I think it must be the new oil he's using in the shop. It is quite strong."

Of course, this was just said for the girls, to appease them. What was actually happening was that Dave had indeed taken to the whisky and was staying out late in the pub or bringing a bottle home with him. Sue had no idea why Dave had taken to drinking. He wasn't the loving man she knew any more. They were growing apart.

"Do you think you and daddy are going to separate?" Alice butted into Sue's thoughts.

"What makes you say that, dear? No, we're not going to separate. Don't you worry, daddy will get over this and will get better. Then we'll be back to our normal family life. I promise."

Oh dear, Sue thought to herself. Children catch on so quickly nowadays. They would have heard Dave shouting at me.

"Look the children are awake." Sue would say in a whisper, "Can't this wait until after they've gone to bed. I don't want them upset, even if you can't be bothered to keep this family together anymore."

"Who's family? They're not mine." He had said a few days ago. Sue decided not to reply. He was drunk and possibly going through some psychological crisis. He looked older, with lines developing around his eyes, and deep chiselled lines on his forehead. His face seemed to be fixed into a permanent scowl and I was beginning to feel afraid of him. Afraid that he'd do something awful. He needed to see a doctor but, of course, he wouldn't go of his own accord and, trying to get a doctor to come out to see someone, was just a pie in the sky dream in the present circumstances, with doctors and juniors striking for more pay and it was bad enough just trying to get an appointment to see a GP, as an outcome of the Covid pandemic. She would have to contact MIND or a similar organisation, or even go private.

Dave had actually moved out to the spare bedroom. Although this was unprecedented behaviour, Sue was wary that he could possibly turn violent in the night and was actually pleased that he had. She found herself locking the bedroom door. She wasn't too worried about the girls as he seemed to be quite alright with them. Also, as Dave was always drunk, the smell was making her nauseous in her advanced state of pregnancy.

Before contacting a doctor, Sue thought she might do some investigation of her own. She decided to go to his works. Surely his work must be suffering and people would have noticed his drinking.

On getting there, Sue saw Dave's works manager, Steve. "How nice to see you here, Sue," he answered. "We don't get to meet up often now, especially with you expecting your third. I expect you've got a lot on your hands, what with your two little girls and the house. Anyway, I'll make you a cup of coffee."

THE ROUGH CLOSE MURDER

"Thanks, Steve. Yes, much appreciated. Yes, I've missed you lot too. I just thought I'd come by to see how things are going. The books seem to show a lot of work going on, and orders."

"Yes, everything's going smoothly, thanks."

Over the coffee, Sue hesitantly proffered a question, "And how's Dave coping? He seems very tired lately and I wondered if he is managing to keep on top of things. I don't know if he's got some sort of a virus."

"Oh, I'm not sure what you mean. Yes, he sometimes looks a bit tired when he comes in. I thought that was maybe not getting enough hours' sleep, what with the remodelling of the house and the two children running rings around him, as they do. But, no, a cup of coffee first thing, as usual, and he's right as rain, ready to go."

"So, he's his normal self?"

"Certainly. You know Dave, a laugh and a joke every minute. He loves these one-liners. What's it he said the other day, oh yer 'I sold the vacuum cleaner the other day - all it was doing was collecting dust." Sue had to laugh. "Yes, Steve continued, "It's a fine workforce we have here and a friendly place to work, but he keeps us all in line. We all know our jobs and we get on with them."

With that, Sue finished her coffee and said she'd not leave it so long to pop in and see him again.

'So, that's strange', she said to herself. 'No mention of Steve rowing with anyone, being in a bad mood, drinking or slacking on the job. Everything there was fine. Oh, I don't understand what's happening. Where do I go from here?'

CHAPTER 14

After receiving the summons, William and John started arguing.

"Eet's oll your woif's fote, John. Susan's allus sticking her nose inte things that dosna concern 'er. Shay mosta riled John sommit terrible fer 'im to come at us loik 'e did."

"She hasna told me exactly what she said, other than trying to give some support and help with his family."

"Aw, yer gone soft int'yed, you, canst look behind 'er words en git the maining?"

"What shay's most likely said is that he's not coping. Mebbee that riled him."

It's all your wife's fault, John. Susan's always sticking her nose into things that do not concern her. She must have riled John something terrible for him to come at us like he did.

Oh, you've gone soft in the head you, can't you look behind her words and get the meaning...... \Maybe that got him annoyed.

"Well, ah thenk theer's mer to it than thut. You know whut shay's loik, loves fancy things. Ah bet shay's got 'er eye on sommit int 'ise, en shay's asked if shay con 'ave eet."

"Well, she did mention that Sarah had some nice objects around th'ise."

"Thut'll bay eet, then. Shay's asked 'im fer sommit en 'es kicked af. 'Es just lost 'is woif. Shay'd no roight, not at funeral! Shay's a cold-hearted kye."

"I willna 'ave you say that abite Susan. She meant no 'arm. She may be tactless somtarms, I grant you that. She just chose wrong moment te ask 'im, when John was naturally in mourning. I'll 'ave a word wi' 'er."

"You do thut. Shay naydes a good thrashing, no just a word! Thenks shay con come en go en do en seey whut she wants, loik royalty or sommit. Yer've marrit a roight hoity-toity pace o' wark."

Well, I think there's more to it than that. You know what she's like... eye on something in the house, and she's asked him if she can have it. That will be it then. Shey's asked him for something and he's kicked off. He's just lost his wife. She had no right. She's a cold-hearted cow. I won't have you say that about Susan. She may be tactless sometimes..... She nees a good thrashing. Thinks she can come and go and do and say what she wants, like royalty, or something. You've married a right peace of work.

THE ROUGH CLOSE MURDER

"If you seey ony more, ah'll stroik you."

"Ah, sev eet fer yer woif."

. . . .

Later on John spoke to his wife, Susan. He wanted to get to the bottom of the argument.

"All I said, after offering any assistance we could give, was that I liked his house and the beautiful ornaments. He must have taken it the wrong way, thinking I was coveting them. I didn't mean to cause offence."

"Well, I think he has indeed taken offence. That's all I can think of as he wouldn't discuss the matter with us. Maybe he overheard you say something?" (Susan didn't like him speaking in the Potteries dialect, wanting him to improve himself, so John tried not to).

"Oh, well, come to think of it, I was talking to Jukes, saying that there seemed to be a poor show of people for the funeral. I wonder if he just overheard part of the conversation – possibly the words 'poor' and 'funeral' or even 'pauper's funeral – as locally that could sound like 'pooer payple'. That doesn't bear thinking about. Oh dear."

If you say any more I'll strike you. Ah, save it for your wife.

"Yes, that could be the answer. With poor John in his miserable state, with the noise of others talking around him, he could have misheard."

"But, why John, dear, did you just not hold him down, after he hit out at you and William. Why did you have to join the fray? Now you have taken out this court summons against him without getting down to the facts, which has led John to take out a cross-summons against the both of you."

"I don't know. He was calling you such names that I felt I had to defend you, and you know William, anything for a fight."

"You've caused more trouble than was started, dear."

"Yes, I know, but that was William's idea."

CHAPTER 15

It was Saturday, 27 February, 1886. After an early lunch, my wife, Susan, William and I were loading the cart up ready to attend Longton market. Our father wasn't going, he had gone to sit in his usual armchair by the fireplace in the living room. He felt the cold these days and his rheumatism was playing up. The pony and trap were ready, the baskets of eggs and butter had been properly packed. It was about 11 o'clock.

We went back inside to get our coats. William sidled up to Susan, meaning to help her with her ulster coat and actually put his hands around her throat. Susan tried to scream, but only a muffled moan came out as William's hands were too tight around her. I turned, and saw her plight and pushed William aside. I then helped Susan adjust her collar but I was seething red.

William shouted out, "Shay'll 'av her collar put roight on Monday (referring to the Court summonses).

She'll have her collar put right on Monday.

"I'll get you for that." I shouted. All the hurt and misery of growing up with this bully of a brother, came flooding back into my mind. I couldn't defeat him then, but I could now. I grabbed the rifle from where it was held in place by a string, over the fireplace and chased after William.

William came hurriedly out of the house by the back door, which led into a paved yard, with me in hot pursuit, carrying the rifle. Susan was immediately behind me.

William was endeavouring to get out of my reach, running through the yard, and had got about twenty yards along the field path, which led directly to the private roadway.

At that point I lifted the rifle to my shoulder, shouting out, "You are not gonna ruin me today." William turned and saw me with the gun and shouted out, "Oh, dunna Jack." I fired – William ducked his head, then ran into the field, trying desperately to escape. I followed, and got ready to take aim again. At that same moment Susan had caught up with me and was trying desperately to stop me but, I pushed her away and, in the struggle, she got an ugly knock on one side of her face with the butt end of the gun and, at that same moment, the gun went off. The charge caught William fair and square by the side of the head and, without uttering a word, he fell to the ground, dead. His head was literally smashed by the charge, his brains

You are not going to ruin me today…. Oh don't Jack.

protruding from the wound. Susan had been knocked virtually unconscious in her attempt to get the gun off me.

I didn't know if I'd actually meant to shoot William or just scare him. "Oh God, I've done it now. There's nowt else for it." I attempted to put the gun to my own head, to blow myself away. I tried to pull the trigger, looping my foot through the attached string, but the trigger just wouldn't pull. It was a waste of time, so I started walking back. Before I knew anything more, father had come out of the house, wondering what all the racket was about with guns going off and screaming. Susan had run up to him screaming, "He's trying to kill himself. Stop him." and father had grabbed the gun off me.

Jukes had been standing about, looking after the horse and cart, and had screamed too. She had seen most of what had happened.

Father, holding the rifle, led me back to the house. Jukes had come running up, "Oh granddad, Uncle John has shot Uncle William." Thomas said nothing, just nodded his head at the poor girl, in acknowledgement.

Several neighbours had accumulated at the scene, having heard the ruckus, and had sent for the Police Constable. The neighbours were causing a great furore with all sorts of discussions on how this possibly could have happened and what caused it. It was about half an hour later when

PC Lloyd arrived as he had been away from home and messages had to be sent to find him.

I suppose I was in total shock. I sat down indoors. I heard someone say I looked very pale. A neighbour, Emma Latham, wife of Henry Latham, and lived near the deceased, had been preparing to go to market herself. On hearing Susan Daniel and Jukes screaming, had gone to investigate and saw William's body, lying in the field.

Thomas Daniel was approaching her, "Oh, John's shot William," she exclaimed, with her hands up at the sides of her face, as an emphasis of the utter shock. Thomas said nothing, just looked at the body. Mrs Latham then went to fetch Mr Gould, another neighbour, then went into the house.

"Oh John, whatever have you been doing?"

I replied, "I have done it, Mrs Latham, and I shall have to suffer for it. William had been upbraiding me about my wife and attacked her. He made a comment about getting her collar being put straight on Monday."

Mr Gould then came in, "Oh, Mr Gould, I knew there had been a 'bother' between the brothers regarding Mrs Bennett's funeral, but I didn't think it would come to this."

THE ROUGH CLOSE MURDER

There was nothing I could do or say, it had been done and there was nothing else to do, but I couldn't just sit there and wait. My blood had turned cold but I was sweating. I was too stressed out. I couldn't sit still. I had to do something. So I seemingly, in a robotic manner, got up and carefully went out again to remove the market baskets from the cart. "Mrs Latham," I called out, "You were on your way to market, can you take our baskets for us please?"

So, John was acting mechanically. The last thing he was doing was loading the cart, so this had to be sorted. The produce had to go to market. At no time did he say he had any regret for what he had done in the heat of his passion. He didn't even mention his brother's name. He was just getting on with something until the police came and took him away.

I couldn't think straight. My mind was a whirl. All sorts of things were going through my brain. How could this have happened? Why did William attack Susan? I didn't mean to shoot him dead, did I? Maybe if Susan hadn't knocked the rifle, William wouldn't be dead now, but I can't blame her, she was just trying to stop me. I had the rifle and I'll have to take the consequences...... What's going to happen now? I'll be hanged. Oh, I wish I was lying dead with William, as I tried, then it would be all over now..... Oh God - I'll never see my little baby."

The local postman, John Duval, was next on the scene and carefully helped to remove William's body into the house.

When in the yard I approached John Duval. "Can you come with me to the police station, John? You live in Stone and, as like as not, I'll be taken there."

John Duval's answer took me aback, "I've nothing to go to Stone for."

I answered, "Well, John, it will, perhaps, be the last good turn you can do for me."- so John Duval agreed.

Susan, in the last stages of pregnancy, the baby being due the following month, was, as you can imagine, in a terrible way, bruised and battered and having to see her husband being carted off to jail, called out, "Can I at least accompany my husband to Stone? I need to be with him. He needs me."

John Duval intervened at this point, "You are in no state to be with your husband. It would all be too traumatic for you and could possibly induce the baby. I cannot allow it."

"That's right," I agreed, and went into the house with Susan, upstairs to one of the bedrooms, to say goodbye to Susan.

"I'm sorry, Susan. I'm sorry William ever came back to the house. If he hadn't been here, this never would have happened. I have to say my goodbyes now. I doubt very much that you will ever see me again, except in Court, when I will be given a date to be executed. I love you Susan, always remember that, and tell our little one, when it is born, whether it be a child or a son, that its father loved it." I think I gave her two watches for her to give to people but I can't remember now, it's all a blur.

I then came down and said my goodbyes to my father and Jukes.

When PC Lloyd arrived, I said to him, "All right, Lloyd, I know what I've done. I shall have to suffer for it. It's done, and it can't be undone. I'll go with you as soon as I have given this watch (which I held in my hand) to Beatrice." I climbed into our own pony and trap and PC Lloyd drove me to Stone. I made no resistance.

On the way I said, "Lloyd, we have all tempers. Some can stand more than others. Will made a remark to my wife about putting her collar straight, and I didn't like it. That caused me to do it."

On arriving at Stone, I saw a man named Albert Lees, and called over to him, "Albert, come and shake hands with me. I've done the deed, he's taken me, and I shall have to suffer for it."

At Stone I was charged and cautioned by the officer with causing the death of my brother. When asked if I had anything to say, I just said, "All right, it is done and cannot be undone."

……………

During this time, the doctor had been called. He examined the body, then turned to the father, Thomas. Thomas was cold and shaking. The doctor was afraid that the shock would have been too great for the father and advised that he should be closely watched.

He also examined Susan, who was having hysterics and crying. He gave her a sedative to calm her and a balm for her face. "It is hoped that she will sleep and be calmer in the morning."

Mr Gould was saying, "How he thinks Susan would be calmer in the morning, knowing that her husband was in jail, having committed a hanging offence, for which he would never be allowed to return, God only knows."

John's wife could not be called to trial due to the present state of the law – at the time a wife could not bear witness for or against her husband.

CHAPTER 16

"May name's not Dave. Dostna even know who yer tokking te? Yer've gone mad int yed. Yer ready fur asylum, you. Ah allus knew yer were a mardy fot kye. Gerr ite o' may feece."

"Dave!"

Susan was frightened. Who was this person facing her? He definitely wasn't her husband. Some sort of force had taken him over.

"Ah telt yer, ah'm no Dave, whoever Dave mebbee."

She was scared he was going to hit her and backed away.

"Why are you talking like that? Where's this old Potteries dialect come from? What's happened to the Dave I know and love?"

May name's not Dave. Don't you even know who you are talking to? You've gone made in the head. I always knew you were a moaning fat cow. Get out of my face.

I told you, I am not Dave, whoever Dave may be.

"Dunno whut yer on abite. In case yer canna rimember, yer may brother John's woif, Susan, Susan Daniel. Best go bek te 'im en 'e con send thee to a mental 'ome, wheer yer belong.

Susan ran out of the house, grabbing her laptop, purse and coat. She didn't know where she was going but just needed to get away. Then she remembered the children. They'd be coming out of school soon and she didn't want them to be confronted by this maniac of a father. So, she went to the school.

"We're going to one of your friend's houses. You can have a stay overnight. That will be great, won't it? You can have an away day, a sleep over."

Emily and Alice were excited.

At the friend's house, Sue had to explain, while the two children met up with the neighbour's children and went to play.

Susan didn't really know what to say. She couldn't tell her the whole truth, as she didn't know what was happening herself.

"I'm sorry to put on you like this, Jean, but Dave is just not well. He's got some sort of bug and I'm frightened the

---

I don't know what you're on about. In case you can't remember, you are my brother, John's, wife. Best go back to him and he can send you to a mental home, where you belong.

children might catch it. I know I'm inconveniencing you in this way but do you think you could possibly have them for a few days? I'll bring a change of clothes for them."

"Oh, that's no problem, Sue. Anything to help. I hope Dave gets better soon."

"Yes, I'm going to get the doctor to him now. I'll be in touch and many thanks, yet again."

As Sue went down the path, she was wondering what her next move should be. Dave didn't need a GP, he needed sectioning.

She was too scared to go back to the house. She'd buy some clothes for the girls. All sorts of things were going through her mind. Should she contact MIND? Should she get a GP to section him? Should she call the police?

Then something dawned on her on what Dave had been ranting on about. He had said that she wasn't his wife and that she was Susan Daniel and that her husband was John Daniel.

After buying a few clothes for the girls and for herself, then taking the girls' clothes to Jean, Sue decided to get a room at the local pub, The George and Dragon. There she set up her laptop and put in 'John Daniels, Rough Close' on Google.

A whole lot of information came up about the Rough Close Fratricide.

In the Staffordshire Sentinel, dated Monday, March 1st, 1886, Sue read:

"A terrible and at present inexplicable act of fratricide is reported from Rough Close, near Longton. The alleged murderer himself sent for the police, and is in custody. The inquest on the murdered man will open tomorrow."

The Newcastle Guardian, dated Saturday, 6th March 1886 read:

"It is a long time since we recorded so dreadful a murder as the fratricide near Longton last Saturday. It is alleged that John Daniel deliberately shot his brother, William, both men in the prime of life, the tragedy taking place near the family homestead at Normacot, and the fatal shot being fired within hearing of their aged father. Perhaps there should be a qualification of the word 'deliberately', for, though the act was determined, deadly and nerveful, the infuriated brother must have been in fierce passion to have committed the deed for which he may have to answer for with his own life. According to Scripture, 'A brother offended is harder to be won than a strong city'; and in this terrible case, a bitter family quarrel seems to have got the mastery over all brotherly feeling. The accused is committed for trial, and at the next Assizes at Stafford, before the tribunal, there he will have to answer to the charge of the highest crime recognised in the land."

THE ROUGH CLOSE MURDER

In the Staffordshire Sentinel, Daily and Weekly (Stoke-on-Trent, Staffordshire) dated Saturday, March 13, 1886, Sue read:

"......The mind's eye has little difficulty in conjuring up the picture – the tiff after breakfast, the lowering brow and angry threats of a man furious with jealousy, unreasoning rage and the irritability which precedes or accompanies insanity, the recourse to violence, the fright of the wife, and the startled screams of the children, but hurried flight into the field, still covered with virgin snow, and the terrible scene that followed, at which it would be well to draw the curtain."

"Hmm, very fanciful and florid writing." Sue thought to herself, "Someone wanted to be more than a newspaper reporter! But there is the gist of it. William and John Daniel did exist and John murdered William on Saturday, 27 February 1886."

There was more, in The Tamworth Herald, dated Saturday, March 6, 1886:

"Shocking Fratricide in North Staffordshire.

A shocking tragedy occurred on Saturday morning at Rough Close, an agricultural village situated midway between Longton and Stone, in North Staffordshire, where a man named William Daniel, aged 42 years, was foully murdered by his brother, John Daniel, aged 36 years. The deceased was a married man, but a few months ago, he separated from his wife and went to live with his father at the Dale House Farm, Rough Close, where his brother John and his wife also resided."

"Oh," Sue exclaimed, "So the murder actually took place at our house!" She read on:

"So far as is known at present, the brothers were living on the most friendly terms, and on Saturday morning, they breakfasted, and afterwards went to work on the farm together. About eleven o'clock, John Daniel returned to the house, and taking a double-barrelled gun, which was kept loaded, proceeded in the direction of the field where William Daniel was working. Going up close behind his brother, John Daniel deliberately pointed the gun at his head and discharged one of the barrels, with the result that the top of the deceased's head was blown off and his brains scattered about. For some reason or other, which has not yet been explained, John Daniel's wife followed him on seeing him take the gun from the house, and she witnessed the murder."

THE ROUGH CLOSE MURDER

"Oh, there's more to this than that. You don't just go out into a field and shoot your brother, after having a peaceful breakfast. No, that's definitely poor reporting." Sue remarked to herself. She finished the report:

"Information of the occurrence was conveyed to Police Constable Lloyd, and having seen the body, he at once arrested John Daniel, and conveyed him to the police station at Stone. On being formally charged with the murder of his brother, the prisoner remarked, 'It was done and could not be undone'.

In the afternoon, the prisoner was charged, before Mr R P Copeland, at Stone, with having wilfully murdered his brother, William Daniel, by shooting him, at Rough Close, the same day. PC Lloyd stated that he was sent for that morning to the Dale House Farm, Rough Close, where he found the deceased in one of the fields He was lying in a pool of blood, and his head had been partly blown away apparently by a gun-shot. He arrested the prisoner, and charged him with having murdered the deceased, to which the prisoner replied, 'It's done and can't be undone'. Upon this evidence the prisoner was remanded, and was conveyed to her Majesty's prison at Stafford.

While being handcuffed at the police station, the prisoner appeared quite unconcerned, and seemed to attach more importance to his father's overcoat which, at the time of his arrest, he had put on by mistake for his own – being returned than to the terrible position he himself occupied."

Sue was deep in thought. "No, it can't be. That couldn't possibly happen - could it? Then again, I've heard of people being possessed by ghosts but Dave seems to have been acting his normal self at work and with anyone he meets. That's not the diagnosis of a drunken tyrant, or some sort of psychological illness affecting his brain functioning, or even emotional reactions and behaviour brought on by stress, or suffering or grief." She looked up mental illness on Google.

"A mental disorder is characterised by a clinically significant disturbance in an individual's cognition, emotional regulation, or behaviour. It is usually associated with distress or impairment in important areas of functioning. Mental disorders are usually defined by a combination of how a person behaves, feels, perceives, or thinks." Then it listed common mental disorders:

Depression
Bipolar Disorder
Dementia
Schizophrenia
ADHD
Autism Spectrum Disorder
Drug and alcohol use disorder
Post-traumatic stress disorder, etc.

"Well, he is definitely misusing alcohol. But, how comes, he is completely sober at work? That doesn't make sense. How can drink get out of his system so quickly?

Yes, it could be bipolar disorder – causing extreme mood swings, but it says here that these mood swings could last several weeks. That doesn't make any sense either. He's not down for some weeks and then up for another few weeks. He's just a different person in the house. He's not like that at work – he's his normal joke-cracking self at work.

What about schizophrenia?" She looked it up. "So schizophrenia includes having hallucinations - hearing voices or seeing things that are not real; delusions – unusual beliefs not based on reality; mudded thoughts; losing interest in everyday activities; not caring about your personal hygiene; wanting to avoid people, including friends. It also says that schizophrenia does not cause someone to be violent and people with schizophrenia do not have a split personality. Ok, what does Google say about split personality? Hmm, it says feeling disconnected from yourself and the world around you; forgetting about certain time periods, events and personal information; feeling uncertain about who you are; having multiple distinct identities; feeling little or no physical pain.

He's definitely in a different time period. He thinks he's in 1886. But, he doesn't feel uncertain about who he is – in his mind he is William Daniel. He's definitely got multiple distinct identities, Dave and William, but I don't know about feeling little or no physical pain - I haven't tried pouring a kettle of boiling water over him, or smacking him around the head with a frying pan or anything to hand - although I'd like to at times. No, I couldn't do that.

Oh, I don't know what to think. It still boils down to Dave being Dave at work, and sometimes this William Daniel comes to the fore at home. I still think it's all to do with the house. We've heard ghosts, someone playing music, the armchair in the living room keeps moving. I've heard movement upstairs when there's no-one in the house. Could it be possible that these ghostly movements and memories have infected the house and, in turn, infected Dave? He may be one of those people who are susceptible to such phenomena.

I want my Dave back." Sue then decided to go onto psychic phenomena in Google. That proved to be a maelstrom of its own – so many people claiming to clean houses of poltergeist and exorcise spirits. Most based their practices on religion, but neither Dave nor I were religious and the sites basically said not to contact them if you were atheist. Others I saw would clean spirits from a distance. I wanted someone fairly local and who would come to the house.

I did find someone in the end, going by the name of Julie Angel. She was based in Malvern in Worcestershire – a bit far away, but not too far. I spoke to her on the phone and told her the basic story. "Don't say any more. Any true medium or psychic would be able to get the information themselves when interviewing the subject. However, I do need to ask you some basic questions." We went through them on various telephone calls – questions such as:

How long we had lived at the property?
What did we both do for a living?
Did I know what was on the land before we bought the house?
Did I know if anyone had committed suicide on the land, or was murdered on the land?
If our relationship was happy.

CHAPTER 17

The doorbell rang. I didn't know what to expect as I had only spoken to Julie Angel on the phone a few times. I suppose I was expecting an elderly, plump dwarf lady, something out of Poltergeist, the film, or someone more resembling a witch in long, flowing, black robes, a long, pinched nose, having knotted black hair and beads.

What presented to me on the doorstep was a quite beautiful, blonde lady, presumably in her 40s, well kempt and well made-up. Behind her were two young, university-type men, wearing jeans and pullovers. They were carrying quite a bit of what looked like electrical equipment. Julie had a suitcase with her.

We introduced ourselves. The two men were James and Robert.

"You know I was going to send my two children to my parents, to be out of the way and because my husband has turned so violent, but you said you needed everyone associated with the house to be present. They are upstairs, playing. My husband is at work at present but will be back later on."

THE ROUGH CLOSE MURDER

"Yes, that's right, Sue. There's quite a bit of preparation to be done before I can start on cleansing a house or an exorcism.

Now, there are a few questions I need to confirm with you first of all. You said, over the phone, that you noticed a change in your husband soon after he had had an electric shock. Now where was he when he was shocked?"

I showed her to the walk-in cupboard by the door.

"Ok, James and Robert, I want you to start setting up your equipment here in this hallway."

She then turned to me, "Before I start any exorcism, the house needs to be completely clean of any forces that may lurk, and that includes you and your children. I hope you have given your house a thorough clean before I arrived, and tidied up, as untidy houses attract ghosts and spirits. The saying, 'cleanliness is next to Godliness' is very true. – oh, not that I am religious or base my work on any religious sect, although I am open to all religions."

I confirmed the girls and I had been busy doing so.

"Of course, when someone rings me up about a possible exorcism, the first thing I have to ask myself is if the subject has a mental health problem, are on drink or drugs, and they are seeing something that isn't really there. I normally ask the caller to direct the subject to his or her doctor first of all.

91

However, I was interested in what you said about Dave only behaving oddly when here, in the house, and that he is his normal self at work. That does not tie in with any mental health issue. He doesn't drink or take drugs, does he?"

"Before Dave changed, we would only have a glass of wine or two, on special occasions, and he has never taken drugs. But now, he's taken to drink in a big way, drinking anything he can get his hands on – vodka, gin, whisky, whatever."

"You tell me he has become aggressive. I will have to tell you that an aggressive spirit or ghost already knows that we are here and that you have called us. They don't want to be removed and they will be ready for whatever I try. I have to be cunning, outfox them, especially the psychopathic ghosts, which I presume this spirit possibly could be.

You say you have also heard movement and sound in other parts of the house. James and Robert will set up their recording equipment where you have heard these noises. I don't think you need fear these entities. They are not actually ghosts but normally a play-back of a possible tragic event, like a movie showing the people and events. They are always dressed in period costume if you see them. What I believe is that these are voices from the past, trying to welcome a lost spirit to the light.

CHAPTER 18

I showed Julie the areas where we had heard ghostly impressions, such as the piano music. I also mentioned various things being moved, such as the armchair in the living room, newspapers, the magnifying glass.

"So, when Dave was working on the electrics, you were at the consumer box and you saw the switch for the hallway turn itself on. Well, that could have been no more than a mechanical fault, but it could have been an entity, a poltergeist. First of all we need to clean the house in every area where there has been interference, shall we say." From her suitcase Julie produced a bundle from a small velvet pouch of what looked like dried leaves. "This is a smudge stick, made of sage, lavender and cedarwood. Sage leaves are considered sacred to Native Americans. It's commonly used for smudging to purify the mind, body and spirit. Lavender has a calming and sedative effect. It helps keep the atmosphere in the property I am cleansing and the occupants calm. It has magical properties of healing, protection and purification. Cederwood brings balance and steadiness to the spirit. It encourages us on our path and help to bring our dreams to reality. Cederwood hold the spirits of the ancients, teaching us to hold fast to the Earth – we don't want Dave going over with William do we?"

I nodded, bemused by what she was doing and enthralled with the information she was relating about the herbs.

While preparing the herbs I say out loud, "With these herbs and salt I purify, protect and renew my purpose that all the deeds performed by me shall be for the good of all. Herbs of Mother Earth and creature of salt I bless you."

Julie continued, "Cederwood is one of the Angelic fragrances. It brings the angels of wisdom closer. I use it for purification and to bring the angels of wisdom to watch over, helping and assisting us when in need, and for their vibration to come closer when the wisdom of the ages is requires."

She also produced incense sticks which she lit and the waft of incense drifted though the rooms. "This incense is not something you can buy in the shops, it is produced to a unique formula with sweet copal, which you probably have not heard of." She then proceeded to set alight the bay leaves in a fire-safe receptacle and let them burn until they were burnt out. She also put salt in a white dish. "This is sea salt and must be left for 24 hours. Sea salt disinfects and purifies whatever it touches and I keep it in a glass container for exorcisms or rituals, spells, magic and the like."

Then she set light to the smudge stick, holding it aloft in her right hand. In her left hand she had what looked like American Native Indian feathers, bundled together. A thick plume of white smoke gradually rose upwards. Julie used the feathers to waft the smoke away from her, into all the corners of each room, at the same time whispering some prayers. "The smudge stick must cover all directions, north, east, south and west, top and bottom."

As she turned to each direction, she was whispering what could have been incantations. "Then we must direct the smudge stick above us," and lifted it high to the ceiling, "then to the ground," lowering the stick to just above the floor. She wandered around the house.

Going to all four corners of every room and while dusting the piano, with the smudge stick, she explained, "Inanimate objects can even hold electrical impressions of times gone by, whether they be positive or negative. It is not always a person, land or building which can be haunted. Are there any other items that were here before you moved in?"

"Yes, the rocking chair in the kitchen and the armchair in the living room."

"Good." And she went with her smudge stick to those items. "And, of course, I will smudge the consumer box, just in case. I see that you have made some changes to the property. Some ghosts do not like changes to be made. They want the place to be as they knew it, and object. About your ghost moving the armchair – that would have been his comfy place, by the fire – but of course, you have boarded up the fire. Touching the armchair, Julie closed her eyes and was silent for a while. "Yes, I can see an old man. His back is bent forward through arthritis. He is reading a newspaper but has a magnifying glass to read the small print, as his eyes are not as they were. Yes, the print in those old papers was extremely small, not like nowadays, and set out in narrow columns. Anyone getting hold of a copy today would have trouble reading the print. I can pick up vibes from objects previously owned – they can even be happy vibes, a wedding ring, for example, of joyous times. But, if the person who owned the object was going through some sort of trauma, if that ring had been thrown in rage, after, say, the marriage had broken up, that will be transposed to the object and anyone wearing it subsequently, would be liable to have bad luck or become ill all of a sudden, even suffer severe depression. If I am rummaging around in a fair or bazaar looking for something interesting, I always feel if I can pick up a vibe from the object. If it is a negative vibe, I immediately, put the object down and do not buy it.

The piano has a good vibe. There were happy times had around it. I can hear people singing. Hopefully, this cleansing, will neutralise the energy."

As Julie was going around the house, she was chanting what seemed like prayers, calling on a supreme being and asking for help to release the spirits in the house. She would wait after every chant as though listening for some response, before going on.

At the rocking chair in the kitchen I markedly noticed Julie take a sharp inhalation of breathe. The room had got decidedly colder and I folded my arms, rubbing them up and down, feeling a shiver down my spine. I hadn't noticed that before and felt slightly alarmed.

THE ROUGH CLOSE MURDER

Finally, Julie held the stick to her heart and, with her Indian feathers, wafted the incense smoke towards her. "So, those are the seven directions, north, east, south, west, top, bottom and within.

"If, after this, Sue, you still experience these phenomena, after this cleansing, I would advise you to burn the items – take them out into the yard and build a bonfire, then scatter the ashes in the sea or a stream, to dissolve them and scatter the forces."

"That will be a shame about the piano. I quite like it and I am also not averse to the music – it is quite comforting at times."

"As you wish, Sue, the energy emitting from the piano is positive and friendly. However, I must tell you that I saw the aura of a man sitting in the rocking chair."

"Yes, I did notice you looked slightly alarmed."

"True. There is a man, haunting this house and I had the distinct impression that he is not someone to be meddled with. He's angry, very angry. Something happened in this room and to that man. I believe he was murdered and his spirit has not gone to the light. We have some work before us, Sue."

When we do the exorcism, I will ask Dave to sit in the rocking chair. In mental institutions, it is quite common to see people in a hypnotic state, rocking themselves backward and forward. It is believed by many medical researchers that babies that were not rocked as a baby or child, have a part of the brain that remains undeveloped. The rocking movement helps trigger a baby's innate calming reflex, a primal neurological response deep in the brain. Adults with depression, anxiety or PTSD often benefit from rocking motions – it's not just mimicking the womb but also releases endorphins – happy hormones! Putting Dave in a rocking chair is ideal once in an induced hypnotics/altered state of consciousness, because the calmer the host is, the more the possessor is going to become weaker. They need negative energy to "survive" on their host."

Julie then walked towards a wall. "So much has changed in this kitchen that it is making it difficult to get an impression of what it used to be like but, I can see a rifle, a rifle used to be suspended on this wall." She then walked towards the kitchen door into the hallway, opened the back door, and walked into the yard. Her pace increased into almost a run. A wall had been built so she could go no further but it looked like she wanted to get into the attached field.

"That field doesn't belong to us anymore, it was sold off a long time ago. But you can open the gate at the end of the yard and get onto the field that way."

Julie followed my directions, getting back to the other side of the wall, then going into the field. She stopped abruptly. "This is where he was shot dead – murdered, with that rifle. Someone, a man, had come out of the house and had chased him, and shot him. There was a woman with him. There had been a struggle. I think she was trying to get the gun off him but, was pushed violently to the ground. The shot rang out. I get the distinct impression that the gun went off accidentally, maybe in the struggle. The man with the rifle is despondent and tries to shoot himself with it….. this whole area will need to be cleansed too, if possible. Land can carry the ghostly recordings from Mother Earth and nature, of all events that have happened there. Those impressions go back through time immemorial, through the rocks and stones and a psychic, such as myself, can read these, like recordings, as though they are being played out in a film in front of me. I have seen battles played out before me at castles I have visited. These recordings cannot be removed, it is the land that is haunted. You can only clear land if it is haunted by ghosts or spirits. You cannot clear the recordings.

CHAPTER 19

We were just going back when Dave drove up.

"What's all this about?" He enquired.

We started talking by the car. I had to think quickly. "Oh, I'm getting the house psychically cleansed – this is Julie Angel."

"Angel, that's an unusual surname."

"Oh, it's actually my middle name but I use Julie Angel as a business name." Dave smiled and they shook hands, then he gave me a kiss on the cheek. Dave was quite pleasant. "Yes, we've had some strange goings on, as I am sure Sue has told you, phantom piano-playing and that armchair that keeps moving. You didn't tell me though, Sue, that you were getting someone in."

"Oh, I thought it would be a nice surprise for you. I was hoping to get it done in just one day, while you were out at work." I thought it best not to elaborate anymore as I didn't want to alarm him with talk about a possible exorcism. In Dave's mind, he was acting his normal self.

Julie then stated, "Don't mind the equipment in the hallway, they are just tools of the trade and I will be packing up now."

Julie had, obviously, picked up on my non-committal attitude, thank goodness. I wanted her to meet Dave and come to her own conclusions.

"How has your day been?" I proffered.

"Oh, the usual. Steve said you had popped in and he told you one of my jokes – probably the one about the vacuum cleaner – yes that was it. So, how's my little baby been doing today?" looking at my very swollen belly and smiling.

"Oh, a few little kicks but, apart from that, he or she has had a pleasant day."

"Anyway, no good stopping here, getting cold. Let's go inside. Can't have my two lovelies getting cold, now can we, and Julie, of course,?"

So, we went through into the hallway to go into the kitchen.

As Dave walked past all the equipment in the hall – all sorts of wire and whistles, including an infrared thermal imagine camera, video camcorder and electromagnetic radiation detector, magnetic field strength meter, laptops and various recording equipment, some of which had been set up on tripods - there was a flash of light and the instruments started registering – needles going back and forth on the meters.

Suddenly Dave gave a sort of growl then started kicking out at the equipment. "Git this jonk ite o' may ise." He shouted in Potteries dialect.

"Just g..go into the kitchen," I stammered, "and I'll get you a whisky."

"Pissing women – en you two lads con scarper too." Shouting at James and Robert, who were trying to get their instruments righted. Dave went to sit in the rocking chair in the kitchen.

Julie followed him through.

She spoke quite sternly to Dave, "Now, Mr Daniel, that is no way to talk to a guest in your house. You are Mr William Daniel, aren't you?"

Dave grunted. "Weer's may whisky?"

Sue appeared with the whisky, which Julie took, then beckoned her to leave the room. Julie continued, "I am Julie Angel. You do not know me, but you seem to be very angry about something. It's no good being angry at me. I would like to talk to you to see if I can help."

Get this junk out of my house. Where's my whisky.

THE ROUGH CLOSE MURDER

"Ay, a reel angel yer looeks too, oll dressed in whait. Whut's yer geem? Best you kaype yer nose ite. Eet's nowt te do wi' you."Julie ignored this and continued, "So, who are you angry with, and I would urge you to be polite, Mr Daniel?"

"Thut woman, Susan, may brother's woif. Shay's nowt but a meddler. Shay should steey ite o' may affeers."

Julie then produced a silver locket on a chain, which she waved slowly in front of Dave. In a slow enunciated voice, "I want you to concentrate on the locket, watch it move from side to side. Watch it until you feel sleepy, then I want you to close your eyes. You are getting tired, sleepy. You're very tired, close your eyes." Dave had closed his eyes. "Now, I want Dave to come to the fore. Is Dave there? Speak to me Dave. Are you there?"

"I'm here." Dave responded very sleepily.

"Now Dave, I want you to listen carefully to what I am saying. You have been infiltrated by someone who used to live in this house, in the 19th century. That person is no longer alive, but his spirit lingers on in this house and has taken hold of your thoughts and actions while you are in this house. We need to get this spirit out of you and send it to the light. Do you understand?"

Yes, you look like a real angel too, all dressed in white. What's your game? Best you keep your nose out. It's nothing to do with you. That woman, Susan, my brother's wife. She's nothing but a meddler. She should stay out of my affairs.

Dave murmured, "I don't understand what you are saying. What do you want me to do?"

"Dave, I need you to be strong. I need you to try to overcome this spirit. You must try to put this spirit into your innermost thoughts and I want you, Dave, to be the dominant soul in your body. When I tell you to wake up, I want you, Dave, to be the person who speaks to me – the person who is in control. Can you do that Dave? Now, when I click my fingers, you are going to wake up and be Dave. I do not want you to go anywhere near the cupboard in the hall. Stay away from there. Stay away from the back door. I want you to ring work tomorrow and say you won't be coming in as there is something you need to sort out. Now, I want you to try your damnedest to ensure the other spirit that has taken your body as a host, will not be able to gain control. Can you do that?"

"I will try."

"Ok, wake up Dave." And Julie, taking the whisky away, clicked her fingers.

Dave, slowly opened his eyes.

"Oh, I think you had a little snooze there, Dave. You must have been hard at work today. You remember me, don't you – Julie. We met outside by your car."

"Oh yes, the ghostbuster. Sorry for falling asleep like that."

104

THE ROUGH CLOSE MURDER

Julie beckoned Sue into the kitchen.

"Oh, lovely. I'm hungry. What's for tea? Oh and Julie, are you staying for something to eat. I'm sure Sue can organise something."

"No, that's fine. I'll be going now, with my two lads, but there is more that I need to do tomorrow, so, if you don't mind, I will leave all of my equipment here for now."

Sue went through into the hallway with Julie. The two lads showed her the 'doorway' on the video that had opened up by the cupboard – a door-shaped continuous stream of flashing light. Sue then went with them to the front door. "Just a minute, I have some more information from the newspapers of the time, about the trial and sentencing of John Daniel." and went to get the paperwork.

"Yes, that will be very helpful. William Daniel will only have a memory up to his death and will not know what happened afterwards. Thank you.

"Before I go, just to tell you that all of you need to take a bath tomorrow morning. Add a teaspoonful of Bicarbonate of Soda plus a cup of Epsom Salts. Add a few drops of a good 100% organic Lavender Oil too. Advise everyone that this has to be a total body cleanse, and they must submerge themselves underwater for at least 10 seconds. I will also take a bath here on my arrival. Tell your family not to towel themselves dry, but to allow themselves to dry off naturally."

MARGARET MOXOM

"But it is cold, Julie."

"Well, please do as I say, unless you have white, freshly laundered towels. It might help you relax if you play some light music and possibly burn a white candle or tea-light. I have anything you might not have if you let me know before I go, including Holy water that I have blessed. I don't know if you saw from my website but I am an ordained Reverend. Pure seaweed, is also effective."

Sue sorted this out with Julie and, with that, Julie said her goodbyes, saying that she would be back the next day.

CHAPTER 20

Julie read the newspaper extracts that Sue had passed to her:

At the Longton police court on Monday before the Mayor and Messrs A Edward and John Aynsley, the summonses in which the murdered man and his brother, the prisoner, were concerned, were called on. The matter was originally before the Court on Monday last, when a summons by John Daniel, the present prisoner, against John Bennett, the brother-in-law of Daniel's, was in the list. Mr Kent, then appeared for Daniel, and Mr Allerton for Bennett. It was stated, however, by Mr Kent that an arrangement had been come to, and the summons was accordingly adjourned for a week. The arrangement, however, was not carried out, cross-summonses being issued by Bennett against both the brothers Daniel, returnable on Monday. Mr Welch now appeared for Bennett and asked, under the mournful circumstances that were known to the Court, that the summonses might be struck out, which was accordingly done.

THE PRISONER CHARGED WITH THE MURDER

At five o'clock in the afternoon, the prisoner was taken before R P Copeland, Esq, sitting at the Stone Police court and charge with the wilful murder of his brother William. The prisoner was remanded and was conveyed to her Majesty's prison at Stafford the same evening. While being handcuffed at the police station, the prisoner appeared quite unconcerned, and seemed to attach more importance to his father's overcoat, which at the time of his arrest, he had put on in mistake for his own, being returned, than to the terrible positon that he himself occupied.

Yesterday, the scene of the murder was visited by some hundreds of persons from the neighbouring town.

The only witness called was P C Lloyd. This officer deposed: "I was sent for this morning a little before 12 o'clock, to go to the Dale House Farm. When I got there, I saw William Daniels in a field, lying on his back in a pool of blood, quite dead. I arrested the prisoner, John Daniels, and charged him with causing the death of his elder brother by shooting him. He said, "All right; it's done, and cannot be undone." The prisoner, in answer to Mr Copeland, as to whether he had anything to ask the witness replied, "He has said nothing but what is right. The prisoner, who seemed unconcerned and indifferent, was then remanded to Stafford Gaol until Wednesday, when he was again to be brought up. At a later hour in the evening he was removed to Stafford in a cab.

CHAPTER 20

(Taken from the Staffordshire Sentinel, Daily and Weekly, Stoke on Trent, Staffordshire – Saturday, March 6, 1886)

On Tuesday 2nd March 1886, in the afternoon, Mr A A Flint, the coroner for the Uttoxeter Division of Staffordshire, held the inquiry, at the George and Dragon Inn, Rough Close, concerning the death of Daniel – Mr Smith (Messrs. Tennant, Paine and Jones, Hanley) appeared on behalf of the prisoner, John Daniel; Mr Hamilton (from the office of Mr G C. Kent, Longton) for the relatives of the deceased, and Superintendent Harston, for the police.

The Coroner, in opening the Inquiry, approached the jury: "You are called to inquire into the death of William Daniel, who has been reported to me as having been shot in the back part of his head, death being instantaneous. The first duty is to go and visit the body." The jury then went and saw the body of the deceased.

When they returned Thomas Daniel, the father of the deceased and the prisoner, a venerable man, about 76 years of age, was called. He said, "I am a gardener and a farmer and I live at Dale House, Rough Close. William Daniel was my son. He was, I suppose, about forty-two years of age. He was a gardener, and lived at Normacot, about three miles and a half from my home. He came to stay with me about three weeks ago, to the best of my knowledge. He came to live with me because trade was slack. I wanted him to help me; he was very useful. He was with me up to Saturday the 27th of last month. I had also a son, named John and his wife living with me. They lived with me regularly. On Saturday morning, they both came into the house, and had their lunch together with me, about eleven o'clock. They were on good terms. Both were dressed for 'going to market'. They were going together – John, and his wife, and William. They were going to Longton market.

John went out first, to the best of my knowledge. William came back for his coat. I said to him, 'Which coat are you going to put on?' And he said, 'This'. I do not know how John got the gun. I know he had it for shooting birds. A few minutes after William had gone out – a very few minutes. I heard the report of a gun. I did not go out. I never stirred until I heard Susan screaming. Before I went out I heard the report of a gun. When I heard it I ran out. The first thing I saw was John and his wife coming down the garden. John's wife said to me, "Oh, dear, he is trying to shoot himself. The gun 'wunner' go off!"

To which the Coroner added, "In my opinion it is very likely indeed that he would try to shoot himself."

The gun wouldn't go off

111

Thomas Daniel continued, "To the best of my knowledge I cannot tell whether I took the gun out his wife's or my son's hand. However, I laid hold of the gun and took it into the kitchen. John never offered to take the gun from me, but he caught hold of me by the shoulder and said, "Oh, father. I'm sorry for you; but you must do the best for yourself you can." Before this a little girl came running up to me – she was holding a horse in the yard – and she said, "Oh, grandfather, Uncle John has shot Will!"

In consequence of what my granddaughter (Beatrice Maud Jukes) told me, I went into the field adjoining my building, and found my son lying dead in a pool of blood, and the cows all around him. They were licking and smelling him. John knew that William came to help me until he got work. John had made a practice of taking my gun out so as to shoot birds. It was always loaded. He was not unaccustomed to a gun. John never made a statement to me as to how William got the gun shot. I have seen John leave the gun in the garden and the stable. I have warned him of this practice, because of the rust. He, however, always brought the gun in at night. The gun produced is my gun. I locked up the gun, then gave it to the police officer. I have had it for many years.

Juror: Did you hear one shot or two shots?

THE ROUGH CLOSE MURDER

Thomas: I heard three reports. The first report I heard seemed to me to be very near. I thought I never heard my gun make such a report.

Coroner: How long was it before the screaming?

Thomas: It was almost after they left the house. It would not be above five minutes after they let the house

Coroner: What is the meaning of that string upon the trigger of the gun? Can you give any explanation at all?

Thomas: I cannot give any explanation of it at all. I could not tell whether it was my gun that went off.

Beatrice Maud Jukes, nine years of age, was called to give evidence. She said: I live with my grandfather, Thomas Daniel. On Saturday last I was holding the trap in which my Uncle John and aunty and Uncle William were going to Longton Market. I saw Uncle William come out of the house to open the gate. Then he came back for his coat, and stood against the gate, and John calling out of the kitchen told my aunt to open the gate. Aunty went to open the gate and Uncle William said to Uncle John, "Come, let us be off." Uncle John then came out of the back kitchen, with a gun, and he said to William, 'Ye bxxxx, ye mean to ruin me today.' He shot at Uncle William, but Uncle William stooped down and he missed him. Uncle William then ran into the field, Uncle John following him. They were then out of sight. I heard John shoot at him –

113

the second shot. I stood holding the horse, and Uncle John came back, coming up the garden. He had the gun in his hand. Aunty went up the garden to him, and I did not see any more. I saw where my Uncle William was lying. I afterward came up for the police."

Coroner: Did William make any remark after John said, "You'll ruin me, you ….."

Beatrice: William replied, "Oh don't Jack!"

Mr Smith: Had you had something to eat with them that morning?

Beatrice: Yes

Mr Smith: Could you see into the kitchen from where you were standing?

Beatrice: I could not see

Mr Smith: How many shots did you hear fired?

Beatrice: I only heard it shoot twice, that is all.

Emma Latham was then asked as a witness: "I am the wife of Henry Latham, and live near the deceased. On Saturday, at about half past eleven, I was going to market. I heard Mrs Daniel and the little girl screaming in Thomas Daniel's garden. I made all the haste I could, and went up to the gate. When there I saw William lying in a field. I went to the deceased and found him dead. The skull was 'blown out'. I then saw old Mr Daniel come up, and he said, "Oh, John's shot William." After I had first brought a neighbour, named Gould, I went away. Whilst in the house with Gould I saw John Daniel. I said to him: "Oh, John, whatever have you been doing?" He replied, "I have done it, Mrs Latham, and I shall have to suffer for it." He also said William had been upbraiding him about his wife. John further said he was helping his wife to put her ulster on and putting her collar straight, and William said, "She'll have her collar put straight before Monday's over." I knew there had been a 'bother' between the brothers regarding Mrs Bennett's funeral.

Note: Collar, Slang: to detain or restrain someone, either physically or figuratively. Against the collar: difficult, exhausting or problematic. The phrase originates from the collar on a horse's harness, which tightens on the horse's neck when it travels uphill. To put someone to shame, to get the better of them.

George Gould, Leydon Dale, was called next. He said, "On Saturday, Mrs Latham came to me about 12 o'clock. I went back with her to Daniels' house. When we arrived there I went straight to the dead man. I then went into the kitchen and found John talking to his wife. John was 'mithering' about dividing 'his things' including two or three watches. He gave Jukes a watch and directed his wife what to do with the others. Previously I asked John "How could you have done it?" John replied, "I felt so mad at him, and was so put about."

The officer came upstairs, whilst they were talking and arrested John.

PC Thomas Lloyd, stationed at Rough Close, said "On Saturday last, about noon, I went to Thomas Daniels' house. On the way I went to the field where the body was lying. I knew the deceased, who was lying partly on his back, with his head in a pool of blood. I felt his pulse, and found that he was quite dead. A portion of his brains was scattered about the ground, a piece of his skull lying about a yard away. I then went to the house, where I saw several people. I went upstairs to the prisoner, who was with his wife in a bedroom. I charged him with causing the death of his brother, William, by shooting him with a gun. I cautioned him as to what he said, saying that what he said would be given in evidence against him on his trial. He said, "All right, Lloyd. It's done, and it can't be undone." I will go with you as soon as I have given this silver watch to Cis," – meaning his niece, Beatrice. I took the prisoner to Stone, and on the way he said, "Lloyd, we have all tempers. Some can stand more than others. It was concerning my wife that caused me to do it. He then mentioned something about a collar. The prisoner, when near Stone, said, 'Lloyd, I'm very sorry for my wife and my father; but it's done and we can't help it.' Afterwards I went to Rough Close and received the gun from the prisoner's father. The left hand barrel had been recently discharged; the right hand barrel being loaded, but with the cap on the nipple. I unloaded the pellet from the muzzle loader and the shot produced was that which I had taken from it. I have since received the shot and powder flask from the prisoner's father. The shot corresponded with the shot produced.

Charles John Gibson said: "I am a Bachelor of Medicine and live at Stone. I first saw the body on Saturday afternoon. I was at Thomas Daniel's. The body was laid out on two chairs. On the right hand side of the head was a shot wound. There was a lacerated wound over the right temple, the bones, and soft part having been carried away. The brain had the appearance of being shot away and part replaced. The skin round the wound in the front part of the head was blackened and scorched with gunpowder – such a wound as would be caused by a shot fired from a gun from a distance of not more than two feet. I looked carefully for shot and found one pellet. That was sufficient to cause immediate death. I have made a post-mortem examination since. I have found that the deceased was a healthy man. There was no cause of death except this wound.

He was asked if he had remarked on the state of John's wife's dress. Mr Gibson replied in the negative but that she had gun powder marks on her face.

The Coroner then summed up at great length, directing his summing up to the jury:

"I do not suppose the jury will require me to read the evidence over. The facts are so simple that you will not have the slightest difficulty in coming to a decision. You are called together to inquire by what means and under what circumstances the deceased came by his death. The history of the whole case appears to be very short indeed. Here was a man who could not get employment, who came to help his father until times were better. William Daniel, until a few weeks back, resided with his wife and family at Normacot. His house, however, being broken up, he went and took up his residence also at Dale House, leaving his wife and children in charge of his son-in-law, who lives at Longton. He came apparently with the knowledge of the other son, and with his desire. There might enter into the minds of some of you that this act would create some jealousy on the part of the other brother, but there did not appear from the evidence to be anything of the kind existing, and the brothers, according to the evidence, appeared to have been on perfectly good terms. It was John's wish that William should come to live at the home again. John had behaved very kindly toward him, and had paid his rent and rates for him, and had bought him some clothes.

Shortly after William's coming back home, a married sister of theirs, named Bennett, living with her husband and children at Normacot, died on the 27th of January in this year, and was buried on the 3rd February. Among outsiders, the general impression seems to be that the murder was the result of a family feud, which commenced at the funeral. At the funeral, Mr Bennett is alleged to have sought a quarrel, which resulted in his receiving a thrashing at the hands of his two brothers-in-law. A summons was taken out against him, and the case was mentioned at the Longton Borough Court on Monday last. It was then understood that the matter was adjourned in order that the parties might come to a settlement. Instead of keeping his promise, the brother-in-law took out cross-summonses against the prisoner and deceased, which were returnable at Longton on Monday. Money matters are believed to be at the bottom of this dispute, but it is difficult to see the connection between it and what occurred on Saturday.

On 27 February, the family lunched together, and John Daniel, his wife and William went out together. When John was putting his wife's ulster on, it appeared that William had made some observation which appeared to have reference to a matter of which we know nothing. It appeared, however to have excited John's temper very much.

As previously stated the brothers, according to the evidence, appeared to have been on perfectly good terms but it is not known for certain that John did not take kindly to his brother's continued presence in the house, and words as a result are believed to have taken place between them. About 11 o'clock on Saturday morning, John Daniel, his wife, and the deceased, were preparing to attend Longton market. The pony and trap were ready, the baskets of eggs and butter had been properly packed, when some disagreement arose between the two men.

The nature of that unpleasantness it is not possible to say. It is alleged by those who were present that what took place did not amount to a serious quarrel. In the face, however, of what so soon happened, this is inexplicable. What was actually known to have occurred was this. William came out of the house by the side door, leading into a paved yard, hurriedly and excited, followed almost directly by the younger brother, his wife and the father. John carried with him a gun. With this he at once made for his brother. John cried out, "You are not going to ruin me today," at the same time raising the gun and firing. That poor fellow endeavoured to get out of his reach. He went through the yard, and got about twenty yards along a field path, leading direct to the private roadway, before mentioned, when the prisoner lifted the gun to his shoulders and fired. The charge caught the unfortunate man by the side of the head and, without uttering a word, he fell to the ground, a corpse. His face was literally smashed by the charge, the brains protruding from the wound.

The prisoner's wife saw the whole occurrence, but cannot be called due to the present state of the law. Her screams attracted the attention of a Mrs Latham, who lived nearby, and the girl, Jukes. The prisoner admitted his guilt to several persons.

The prisoner's wife and his father did their best to avert the catastrophe, and in the struggle, which ensured, the woman got an ugly knock on one side of her face with the butt end of the gun, from the effects of which, it is asserted, she became, for a short time, insensible.

Many rumours are afloat with reference to the crime and the characters of the two men are being somewhat roughly handled. Much that is said about both, of course, will not bear repeating. There is, however, little doubt that the man now in custody is remarkable for his hasty temper and perhaps was not too particular in either what he said or did. He nevertheless, is a shrewd business man and is believed to be in a prosperous condition, so far as his finances are concerned. He bears a better character than the man whose life he has taken. He is thirty-six years of age. The murdered man has got his living in recent times as a journeyman gardener. He was forty-two years of age, and leaves a widow and six children. It is remarkable that his widow was widowed when he married her, her first husband meeting with as sudden, though an accidental end. He, in fact, fell out of a cart and broke his neck. William has been in the hands of the police. He was, unfortunately, given to drink, and had his home sold from him.

However, if a man fired a gun at another and killed him, the jury have the right to assume that, at the time, he intended to do it, and I think the jury would not have the slightest difficulty in saying there was malice prepense. It is not for the jury to inquire into the state of the mind of the murderer at the time. Nevertheless, bear in mind that the ramrod and the powder and shot flask remained in the house all the time until the father put them in the stable.

The jury, having considered their verdict in private, returned a verdict of WILFUL MURDER, against John Daniel.

CHAPTER 21

(Taken from The Staffordshire Sentinel Daily and Weekly (Stoke-on-Trent), Sat, Mar 6, 1886)

On the Wednesday, a special Magistrate's Court was held at the Court House, Stone, before Mr J F Wileman, for the purpose of hearing the examination of the prisoner, John Daniel, charged with the wilful murder of his brother, William Daniel, at Rough Close on Saturday morning last. The Court was crowded.

Mr Smith (Messrs. Tennant, Paine, and Jones) appeared on behalf of the prisoner and Superintendent Harston conducted the prosecution on behalf of the police.

During the examination, which was necessarily of a formal character, the evidence given at the inquest being repeated with scarcely any variation, the prisoner maintained a cool and somewhat impassive demeanour. He has an intelligent countenance, but his mental organisation, as denoted by his lowness of forehead, strikes a spectator as being defective. He paid close attention to the evidence, and once made an audible comment on something stated by one of the witnesses, but this did not prevent him from frequently scanning the

Court, when he returned the curious glances of the auditors with perfect unconcern.

The first witness called was the prisoner's father, Thomas Daniel, market gardener and farmer, who repeated evidence similar to that he gave at the inquest on Tuesday. Witness added that, after he had been in the field and seen his son lying there, he returned to the house. He saw John and his wife coming out of the garden down some steps which lead to the back door. John's wife, told him "He could not shoot himself because the gun would not go." They were carrying the gun and Thomas Daniel took it from one of them, but he would not say which. They all went into the kitchen, and then John said, "Oh father, I've done it. I am sorry for you." Thomas Daniel locked the gun up in the stable, and afterwards, on the same day, handed it to P C Lloyd. John also said to Thomas Daniel, "You must do the best you can for yourself." Thomas Daniel identified the gun produced and stated that he had not noticed the string on the trigger. As far as he knew, his sons were on the best of terms, but John was passionate.

Cross-examined by Mr Smith, Thomas Daniel said John was agreeable that William should live with him. William was poorly off, but it was his own fault. The week before John had paid a poor-rate of about £1 for him. John had also bought William a pair of boots seven or eight days before the occurrence. The gun was always kept loaded, over the mantel-shelf, and John had been in the habit of using it almost every day. The gun was kept in the room where they had lunch, but it was not there when John went out. Thomas Daniel had frequently cautioned John about his passion. He did say, "Oh, father, I've done it!"

Thomas Daniel's witness evidence, as having a most important bearing on the case, was listened to with the keenest interest, and a good deal of commiseration was felt for the aged man, bent almost double with years and hard toil, narrating the facts known to him.

The other witnesses were Beatrice Maud Jukes, Emma Latham, George Gould, Lloyd (the policeman), and Dr Gibson, all of whom repeated their evidence as given at the inquest.

At the conclusion, the prisoner was formally charged by the Clerk, and reserved his defence, after which he was committed for trial at the Assizes, for wilful murder.

CHAPTER 22

At the Stone Assizes held on 8 May 1886 John Daniel (35), described as a labourer, was arraigned for the wilful murder of his brother, William Daniel, at Rough Close, on February 27. Mr G Gumbleston and Mr R Smith were for the prosecution: Mr J Underhill Q C, with Mr H T Boddam, defended the accused.

The learned counsel for the prosecution, on opening the case, said that the facts were extremely simple, and he thought they would have no alternative but to find the prisoner guilty of the grave charge for which he was indicted. It appeared that the prisoner and the deceased resided with their father, Thomas Daniel, who was a farmer and market gardener, living at Dale House Farm, Rough Close. Besides these, the prisoner's wife and an orphan girl named Jukes, also lived there The deceased had been living away from his father, but about three weeks before the occurrence, he came back, leaving his wife and children with friends at Longton. There did not appear to have been any quarrel or enmity between them, and they would have to form their own opinion what led to the sad occurrence. Shortly after William's coming home, a married sister of theirs, named Bennett, died, and the prisoner seemed to have made the arrangements for the funeral, which, however, did not give satisfaction, and a quarrel ensued between the brothers and Bennett, which led to fighting. Cross-summonses were issued in consequence, which were to have been heard on 22nd February, but were adjourned until the 29th' they were not, however, heard on account of the deceased meeting with his death in the interval. On the morning in question, the prisoner, deceased, and the prisoner's wife, were going to Longton market. The deceased and prisoner's wife were waiting for the prisoner. The prisoner came out with the gun, and said "You are going to ruin me today", at the same time raising the gun and firing. The deceased 'ducked' his head, and then ran out of the yard into a fields. The prisoner followed, and fired again. The shot took effect, blowing the deceased's brains out. The prisoner's wife, it would appear, saw the whole occurrence, but still, under the present state of the law, could not be called. Her screams attracted the attention of a Mrs Latham, who lived near, and the girl Jukes. The prisoner had practically admitted his guilt to several persons.

Thomas Daniel, father of the prisoner, deposed to being in the house on the morning in question On hearing a shot, went out, but could see no-one at first. Afterwards, he found his dead son in the field. He then returned to the house, and subsequently met the prisoner and his wife coming out of the garden. One of them was carrying the gun, but he could not say which. He took the gun and put it in the stable. The prisoner's wife told him what had happened, and that the prisoner had attempted to shoot himself, but the gun would not go off. When they went into the house, the prisoner said, "Oh father, I've done it! I couldn't help it; you must do the best you can for yourself."

Cross examined by Mr Underhill, the witness said that the prisoner and deceased had always been on friendly terms. It was the prisoner's wish that William should come to live at the home again. The prisoner had behaved very kindly towards him, and paid his rent and rates for him, and had bought him some clothes. He added that the ramrod and the powder and shot flask remained in the house all the time until Thomas Daniel put them with the gun in the stable.

Beatrice Maud Jukes said she was a grand-daughter to Thomas Daniel and was ten years old. On the morning of the 27th February she was holding the pony at the house door. Her Uncle William, the deceased, was in the yard, and her aunt, the prisoner's wife, had gone to open the yard gate. Her Uncle John came out of the house with the gun and, addressing William said, "You are going to ruin me today!" He then ran him down the yard. She heard her Uncle William say, "Oh, don't, John!" Beatrice Maud Jukes gave her evidence very reluctantly. She said at first that she did not see John do anything to make William say, "Oh, don't". Being repeatedly questioned, she admitted that she saw the prisoner point the gun at the deceased, but added "He did not fire it" – his lordship reminded her of the evidence she had given before the coroner and the magistrates to the effect that she saw the prisoner fire. She now said she did not know what they meant. She admitted that the cap 'flew off', but would not say that the prisoner fired it.

The Judge: Did you see any smoke?

Jukes: Yes. I saw a bit of smoke.

The Judge: Where did it come from?

Jukes: It came from the cap.

The Judge: Snapping does not make smoke. Has anybody been saying anything to you yesterday?

Jukes: No

Emma Latham, wife of Henry Latham, deposed to being on her way to market on the date named, when she heard screams proceeding from Daniel's garden. She went there, and saw the deceased lying on his back, quite dead. She then went to fetch George Gould. On her way she saw the prisoner under the bush at the top of the garden, with the gun in his hands. She heard the snap of a cap. When she got to the house, the prisoner and his wife and Thomas Daniel were there. She heard the prisoner say that he had done it, and must suffer for it, but he (the deceased) had aggravated him to it. The prisoner further stated that, in the morning, whilst helping his wife with

129

her ulster, and putting her collar right, the deceased said, "She'll have her collar put right on Monday."

George Gould gave corroborative evidence.

Police-constable Lloyd, stationed at Rough Close, deposed to going to Daniel's house on the date named. He found the deceased lying in a field, quite dead. The right-hand side of the forehead, and the back part of the skull were blown away, and his brains were scattered about the ground. PC Lloyd then went to the house and arrested the prisoner on a charge of causing the death of his brother. The prisoner said, "All right, Lloyd; I know what I've done. I shall have to suffer for it. It's done, and it can't be undone. I'll go with you as soon as I have given this watch (which he held in his hand) to Beatrice." On leaving the house with PC Lloyd, John wanted to go by the field, but PC Lloyd declined to go that way. John said, "But Will isn't dead, is he?"

Mr Underhill, QC: Just to confirm, the prisoner actually said "But Will isn't dead, is he?"

PC Lloyd: That is correct, milord.

Mr Underhill, QC: Please continue PC Lloyd.

PC Lloyd: On the way the prisoner said, "Lloyd, we have all tempers. Some can stand more than others. Will made a remark to my wife about putting on her collar straight, and I didn't like it. That caused me to do it." On arriving at Stone, the prisoner called to a man named Albert Lees, saying, "Albert, come and shake hands with me; I've done the deed; he's taken me, and I shall have to suffer for it." PC Lloyd received the gun from Mr Daniel; the right-hand barrel was loaded; the left-hand barrel was unloaded; there was no cap on either.

Sampson Lloyd, landlord of the George and Dragon Inn, said he was in the Stone Road, near Dale House. He heard two shots from a gun, followed by screams. He ran in the direction and found the deceased on the ground. He then went for the policeman.

Mr Charles J Gibson, surgeon, Stone, said he was called to see the deceased on the day named. Death had resulted from a gunshot wound, by which part of the skull was blown away. He should say deceased was fired at from the front, and the distance of the muzzle of the gun from the deceased's head would be about two feet.

Mr Underhill then addressed the jury for the defence. He said the facts appear simple, almost cruelly simple, but there was something beneath the outer crust of the case, which was not apparent to them. He pointed out the absence of any motive, and asked them were they prepared to believe that there were two shots fired. Beatrice at first said there were, but now said there were not and possibly she was mistaken at first. He pointed out that only one shot was fired, from the fact that Thomas

131

Daniel had proved that the ramrod, and powder and shot flasks remained in the house all the time, and one barrel was loaded when it was handed to the police constable. Suppose there had been a shot fired, he argued that, if the prisoner had been actuated by a murderous purpose, he could easily have shot his brother down in the yard. He suggested that the whole affair appeared rather the set of a man wishing to frighten his brother, on account of his having insulted his wife. He thought the facts bore out this view, as it appeared that, even while chasing his brother down the field, he did not shoot him.

As it appeared from the surgeon's evidence, the deceased was shot from the front. In all probability, what occurred then was that Mrs Daniel, hearing hurried steps behind her, turned round, and saw her husband flourishing a gun in front of the deceased. Fearing some disastrous occurrence, she took hold of the gun or the man's hand to prevent this; but the gun went off and shot the deceased. It was certain that she must have been pretty close to the weapon, as the surgeon proved that she had shot marks on the face. As to the prisoner's statement, he urged that these were quite as consistent with expressions of remorse at what had accidentally happened as with admission of his guilt.

The jury then retired to consider their verdict. After an absence of nearly two hours, they returned into court with a verdict of manslaughter.

THE ROUGH CLOSE MURDER

His Lordship, in passing sentence, said he could not conceal from himself that the prisoner had shot his brother in a most furious temper. His life had been saved by the verdict of the jury, but he must be severely punished. He would be kept in penal servitude for 20 years.

CHAPTER 22

Julie came out of the bathroom wearing a long white cotton, flowing gown and white, leather shoes. Julie told Sue to change into something white too, if possible, anything that is of natural cloth, so no nylon.

Sue approached her, "I'm really not sure about this, Julie. I mean that Dave has been fine since you left. Maybe the entity has left him and we do not have to go through this exorcism."

"Dave is only hypnotised, Sue. The entity has to be cleansed from his body. I am going to do my best to do so, but you must expect this spirit to be cunning and conniving, especially if they are psychopathic, as I believe William Daniel may have been. William will know I am here and that I want him to leave. But he may not want to leave and might try anything he can to stay. 99% of my exorcisms are successful but I must also warn you that there is that 1% chance that the entity will return.

Dave was asked to sit down in the rocking chair in the kitchen. She spoke to Sue, "I'm putting a circle of protection around Dave, you and myself. I am going to call on Jareek, my Native American Indian Guide and two Roman Gladiators to protect me.

Sue didn't know what to think of this, were two gladiators and an American Indian going miraculously to appear in

134

her kitchen? Her second thought was, is there room for everyone? She was excited but, then again, very worried and getting even more anxious the more she thought about it. She'd never seen an exorcism in real life and the only ones on the TV called on the Catholic Church to perform the ritual, such as in The Exorcist and the Exorcism of Emily Rose. Both of which were exhausting and went on for days, even weeks, with the body of the person who had been taken over, being wracked with pain and wounds. not to mention the body of Regan in the Exorcist, having her head revolve 360 degrees, drooling out profanities through a green bile and killing the priest. Oh no, what have I got Dave into? She was just about to shout out to Julie to stop, but Julie was in her own world, as though mesmerised.

Julie was chanting, "Dear God, Great Spirit, I gratefully and respectfully request that you draw close to guide and protect myself, Dave, Sue, James and Robert during this exorcism, for the Greater Good of all. I ask you to protect the body of Dave, but not the entities that do not belong."

The atmosphere in the room changed. The room went cold.

"No stop" Sue called out. "I don't know what I've got myself into. Is Dave going to be harmed? You haven't told me what to expect or how long this is going to go on for, please stop."

Julie stopped immediately and turned towards Sue, "As I have said there can be some disruption, the spirit may turn nasty and I have to be on my guard. But I have my protective circle and my guards. Nothing will happen to Dave. I can't say exactly how long this procedure will take, it all depends on the strength of the spirit, but normally I can direct the spirit to the Light fairly quickly. They know when they are beaten."

Sue was becalmed a bit by this, but then added "But what about this guards you mentioned. Will they actually materialise, here in this kitchen? There won't be room for everyone. "

Julie had to smile, "My dear Sue, my Roman Soldiers, or 'gladiators' as I call them, will only materialise to me. You will not be able to see them. I'll describe them for you. They are tall, with a red plume on their silver helmets, and they wear metal breastplates. They also have a shield and sword, a metal-type skirt with material underneath and open sandals on their feet. The image is actually comes from Christianity – Pauls letter to the Ethesians, where he says, 'Put on the whole armour of God that you may be able to stand against the wiles of the devil'. Then he says, 'Put on the breastplate of righteousness, take the shield of faith and take the helmet of salvation and the sword of the Spirit, which is the word of God'.

As you know, I'm not of any particular faith, but these soldiers do appear before me to protect me. They appear and stand one either side of me, like guards in a sentry box. Their duty is to stand guard and prevent the passage of unauthorised souls/entities, demons and so forth getting at me. They guard and protect me, but not anyone else in the same way. Jareek is 'my' spirit guide, so he guides me – not anyone else. I guess it's like having my own cavalry on board if you will!

Of course, they only protect me from a volatile spiritual or otherwise scenarios – though they are not as clever at diverting flying objects, hence a black eye I received one time from a poltergeist incident, throwing something at me. I'm not too good at dodging flying objects, but that was a lesson for me in how powerful these entities can be.

The Armor of God

Helmet of Salvation

Breastplate of Righteousness

Finally, my brethren, be strong in the Lord and in the power of His might. Put on the whole armor of God, that you may be able to stand against the wiles of the devil . . .

Sword of the Spirit

Belt of Truth

Stand therefore, having girded your waist with truth, having put on the breastplate of righteousness, and having shod your feet with the preparation of the gospel of peace; above all, taking the shield of faith with which you will be able to quench all the fiery darts of the wicked one. And take the helmet of salvation, and the sword of the Spirit, which is the word of God; praying always.

EPHESIANS 6:10-18

Shield of Faith

Shoes of the Gospel of Peace

So, if you are happy, I'll proceed."

As Dave was still hypnotised, she clicked her fingers to release him.

"Who am I speaking to?" she said projecting her voice powerfully.

"William Daniel", he shook his head as if to waken up. "Ah, eet's you agin. Migh, dosna shay look pretty – Angel by name en shay looeks just loik an angel, all in woit. But yer no an angel – yer flish and boon. Whut ah'd loik te do wi' you, just neow. Yer look roip fur the tekking."

Then he got up from the chair and walked slowly towards Julie, his hands raised at throat level.

"Sit back down, this minute Mr Daniel. Now." She said, loudly and confidently.

He staggered back but then said, "Nah, ah'm gonna 'av yer." And proceeded forward again.

"Supreme Being, protect me." She called out.

Ah, it's you again. Migh, doesn't she look pretty – Angel by name and she looks just like an angel, all in white. But you're not an angel – you're flesh and bone. What I'd like to do with you just now. You look ripe for the taking. ...No, I'm going to have you.

139

As William came forward, his hands about to haul her towards him, there was a flash of light, electricity, and William was thrown backwards.

"Ah, yer no gonna pleey fair. Yer 'ere to git red o' me, ah know. But ah'm no goin' that aysy. Yer think ah'm just a warthless dronk but this is may 'ise en ah'm goin' nowheer.

You lessen te may. Eet's you who naydes to go." And he shouted, "GEER ITE O' MAY 'ISE."

Julie then beckoned her two lads to tie William down to the chair. William wasn't having that and the two lads had a right job on their hands, fending off fists and kicks. William was screaming a lot of abuse, "You stinking whore" and such like.

They succeeded in the end in taping him to the chair, having to resort to hitting him over the head and virtually knocking him out. Sue was looking on in terror, a hand over her mouth, trying not to scream. That was her husband's body being beaten…. but it wasn't him.

"You will calm down Mr Daniel." Julie said calmly but forcefully. "If you calm down and listen to what I have to

---

Ah, you're not going to play fair. You're here to get rid of me, I know. But I'm not going that easy. You think I'm just a worthless drunk but this is my house and I'm going nowhere. … You listen to me. It's you who needs to go. Get out of my house.

say, you can be untied." She continued, "You are more than you remember, and you have the power to choose, and there is a place of Light and love where you belong. Even the darkest soul can make a new choice and take steps to return home to the Light. This choice is always, always, open to your soul."

William was slumped in the chair, groaning.

Julie then turned to Sue. I can see the aura of William Daniel in a sort of projection over your husband's form.

He has oily dark-hair but with grey at the sides. .I know he is 42 but he looks older. He had a low forehead with his hair falling over it. He is tanned and muscled. I believe he is shorter than your husband – about 5ft 6 inches. His hands are large and calloused. He is grimacing at present, but he is hurting. His forehead is heavily lined, his nose is straight and he has full lips. He is developing a beer belly. He has green eyes."

Sue replied, "Yes, nothing like Dave. As you know, Dave is quite tall, with fairish hair and is 32, quite handsome features and a slim build. Dave has blue eyes and quite average lips, not full.

William appeared to be coming round so Julie continued, "William Daniel, you were killed by your brother, John, in 1886 – he shot you. That was over 100 years ago. I will show you a newspaper, so you can see the date at the top."

MARGARET MOXOM

On seeing the date, there was a shocked look in his face but then said, "Thut's all loyse. Yor've got someone te print thut 'specially te desave me."

"Look around Mr Daniels. Have you seen a kitchen like this? Is this your kitchen? Your kitchen, remember, had wooden beams and a wood-filled oven, with old blackened pots and pans hung around it. There was an old wooden table in the centre and chairs with curved backs. Where's the old sink gone to? Can you see the light above you? That's electric, powered by an on and off switch on the wall." - one of the lads turned the light on and off."

"Ah saey nowt. Ah saey may farm'ise as eet wus en is. Yer doin' majeek. Yer canna fooel may.Yer nowt but a weetch."

Julie said to the others, "So, he can see the new kitchen, through Dave's eyes, but that's superimposed by his memories of how it used to look."

"Mr Daniel, do you remember running into the yard and into the field, being followed by your brother, with the rifle?"

That's all lies. You've got someone to print that, especially to deceive me. I don't see anything. I see my farmhouse as it was and is. You're doing magic. You cannot fool me. You're nothing but a witch.

142

THE ROUGH CLOSE MURDER

"Yer, ah rimember. Ah'd taunted him abite 'is woif, Susan. Ah sayed shay'd 'av 'er collar felt on Monday at cross-summonses.

'E didna loik eet, en got rifle af woll. I ron inte yard. 'E fayred en ah docked. Thut consaited woif o' 'is, kem running efter 'im. Ah canna bear 'er."

"Do you remember anything after that?"

"Nah, spose way med op."

"Do you remember the outcome of the cross-summonses?"

"Nah." and he looked a bit perplexed.

"Surely the cross-summonses meant a lot to you. You wanted to see Susan be brought down –to be observed as being behind the quarrel?"

William said nothing.

"The reason you cannot remember is that John shot you dead in that field. You are haunting this house, William."

Yes, I remember. I'd taunted him about his wife, Susan. I said she'd have her collar felt on Monday at the cross-summonses. He didn't like it and got the rifle off the wall. I ran into the yard. He fired and I ducked .That conceited wife of his came running after him. I can't stand her... No, I suppose we made up.

143

"You've 'aving a laff, duckie. John's too sceered o' hinsel te shooet may." and he guffawed.

"John was sentenced and was jailed for 20 years."

Silence

"Can you see John here, or your father Thomas? Are they with you in this house?

Silence. William slowly started rocking in the chair.

Julie continued, slowly but emphatically, "The Divine Light has already forgiven your spirit for what has happened and there are loved ones in the Light waiting to welcome it home. Your loved ones are waiting for you to join them, waiting on the other side. I can bring them here to escort you to the light. You will not be alone. Your father and mother will be there by your side. Do not be afraid of moving on. There you will have a new beginning. You can start again. I won't let anything harm you. I will protect you as you go to the light."

"OK, ah wunt te mooeve inte loit."

"That's good, William. I can start the process." and she told the lads to release William from his bonds.

As soon as he was released he stood up and looked

You're having a laugh, Duckie (a Potteries greeting). John's too scared of himself to shoot me… OK, I want to move into the light.

around the room. His eyes fell on Sue. "Thut's the betch, 'er wi' John's kid int bally. Eef ah'm dead, thut's the betch thut killed me, nut John. Eet wus 'er oll along shoved gun so John fayred direct at may. It was 'cos o' 'er why theer wus no brass te git may bek on may fayte. Shay'd spint it oll. Eet wus 'er cosed rockus at funeral, tha knowst. Shay boggert may op gooed en proper. Shay dosna deserve te lev."

At this, William made a lunge for Sue. Sue screamed. Next second he had his hands around her throat, squeezing tightly. James and Robert jumped to her rescue trying with all their might to get Sue free, but he was so strong, and pushed them both off.

William was growling. James hit him over the head with the nearest heavy object to hand, which happened to be a frying pan, but that just stunned him. Sue was sinking to the floor, not able to breathe.

Julie called to the Supreme Being. "PROTECT SUE." and threw holy water onto William's back and neck. Flashing bands of electricity struck William and he yelped, but still

---

That's the bitch, her with John's kid in her belly. If I'm dead, that's the bitch that killed me, not John. It was her all along shoved the gun so John fired direct at me. It was because of her why there was no money to get me back on my feet. She'd spent it all. It was her who caused the ruckus at the funeral, you know. She buggered me up good and proper. She doesn't deserve to live.

clung on, but weakened, and James and Robert managed to force him away and bind him up.

Sue was left in a choking heap on the floor, shaking like a leaf, desperately trying to get her breathe.

Julie then called for a Master from the Light Realm. "Come and help me to help the lost entity, and take him to the Light."

She addressed William, "This lady is not John's wife. She is Dave's wife, the body you are controlling." Then more forcibly, "I DEMAND THAT YOU LEAVE DAVE'S BODY. LEAVE THE BODY OF THIS MAN..... YOU ARE NOT OF THIS EARTH. YOU DO NOT BELONG HERE."

Julie then invoked Angelic beings to create a vortex for which William's soul could pass through, "Archangel Michael, Archangel Michael, Archangel Michael, I gratefully and respectfully request you use your almighty sword to cut the cords that bind the soul of William Daniel to the earth plain. I gratefully and respectfully request this NOW for the Greater Good of ALL. I ask this in love and light, love and light, love and light.

Archangel Raphael, Archangel Raphael, Archangel Raphael, I gratefully and respectfully request you surround your healing energy of emerald green light to heal Dave, the soul of William Daniel and all who enter and reside in this property. I ask this in love and light, love and light, love and light.

THE ROUGH CLOSE MURDER

Archangel Gabriel, Archangel Gabriel, Archangel Gabriel, I gratefully and respectfully invoke your brilliant white light and Angelic Wings to illuminate, cleanse, purify and harmonise Dave, the soul of William Daniel and all who enter and reside in this property. I ask this in love and light, love and light, love and light.

Then to everyone gathered there, "Everyone, close your eyes and tune into the energy. I have called for the Master of the Light Realm to guide this spirit home."

Shortly the atmosphere in the room became calmer, and there was a sudden rise in temperature. "Do you feel the presence? The Master is here."

She then looked at Dave, who seemed peaceful now. "I am going to wait with you now while your father and mother come for you – Thomas and Sarah Daniel. You will not be alone. Do not be afraid. You are safe. They have been waiting to see you again. You will feel their spirits when they arrive. It won't be long now. Once your mother and father are here, they will know what to do. You will be accepted in the afterlife. When they are here, you will feel uplifted."

A feeling of peace came into the room, a feeling of relief and even happiness.

They watched Dave, who seemed to have fallen into a sleep.

James and Robert had brought their infrared cameras into the kitchen to film the event. They had already protected them by encasing them in clear quartz, labradorite and selenite crystal as an exorcism would drain the electricity from them, without protection, and they would be rendered useless. On the screens they could see two smoke-like layers bearing a semblance of human forms, moving towards Dave, and another rising up from his supine body. They watched as the three forms glided out of the kitchen into the hallway, then through the glowing portal. Then, quick as a flash, the portal had gone. Everything was back to normal.

CHAPTER 23

Robert and James rushed to untie Dave from his bonds and bring him to a seated position. He was groggy but managed to stand up.

Julie was saying more prayers, to thank the spirits who had helped in the exorcism.

"We must now leave an offering to the spirits as a thank you. Sue, bring the children in for this." Sue called for them to come down. They looked a bit bemused but followed Julies instructions. "I want you all to join together, holding hands and give thanks. Repeat after me: We thank the Supreme Being and the Universe for this assistance." Julie then lit a candle. A flower from the garden would have been appropriate, but it was February, so not much in bloom. Instead, she put a drop of rosemary oil in an abalone shell. "This is a thank you gift to the spirits who helped, the Supreme Being, Thomas and Sarah Daniel, for the assistance that has been given." She then sprayed a fragrance into the room, saying "Bless the Earth" then to all of us, "This is my own personal thank you gift, as an Earth blessing."

"I must now bless the land, although, as I have told you, the recording of the event will always be there." Before she went she told us, "Once the clearance is complete I'd advise you not to talk about the incident, as talking about the entities strengthens them and can bring them back. The best thing you could do is to invite friends round and have a party. Don't tell them why. I mean, you haven't been here long, so say it's a house-warming. This will put your energy back into your space."

In the meantime, and while James and Robert were getting their instruments packed up, Sue and Dave had a bit of time to themselves. Sue was still physically shaking. She tentatively stepped towards Dave to give him a hug – that would have been what she normally would have done before, if he'd been stressed out, but looking at him, she found she couldn't bring herself to do so. Dave gave Sue a hug instead, but she didn't reciprocate with a kiss. "I'll make a drink", she found herself saying, to break the obvious tension. She was going to make a coffee but decided that might not be the best thing. She needed something calming and decided on a camomile tea. Over the tea Dave talked about how he felt. "It's a strange feeling. I feel somehow at peace, as though a great weight has been lifted off my shoulders, although my head is pounding – did I hit my head? Anyway, I feel lighter, calmer and strangely happy."

"Yes, those lines around your eyes, have disappeared now, and your lovely blue eyes are sparkling again, not the green eyes of William Daniel. It's good to have you back." the tea was calming her. "I must ask you though, did you have any recollection of how you were behaving, the excessive drinking for one?"

THE ROUGH CLOSE MURDER

"I knew, but it was as though I had no control. I had no control of what I was saying or doing. This other being stopped me being me. It was as though I was in the background, looking through a glass window and shouting, but no-one could hear me. The only time I was myself was when I was out of this house."

Sue suddenly blurted out, "You frightened me, Dave. I'm sorry, but it has to be said. I was scared for my life and you actually tried to kill me at the exorcism, and almost succeeded if it hadn't been for James and Robert and what Julie called the Supreme Being. Do you remember any of that?"

"I'm sorry, Sue, really sorry, but this thing had such a hold on me. It wasn't me, you have to believe that."

"I know, and I'm really trying hard to get round it. It's going to take me some time to know that my husband's hands were trying to suffocate the life out of me. It's your picture in my mind, not this William Daniel. It was your face."

"Oh love, what can I do, what can I say?"

"Another thing I remember Julie saying, was a clearance or exorcism is only 99% successful, which means that there is that 1% chance that this will all happen again, and all this about not telling anyone about it – I mean, what if the girls want to – need to – discuss what has gone on?"

"Oh but 1% is such a minute chance, Sue."

"I really don't know. I'll have to think it all through…..
I really don't want to be put through all that again……
I want to leave this house, Dave. Just sell up and leave."

"But, we've put our whole savings into this place."

"I don't care. I've made up my mind. Sell up and move
away from the whole area."

"You won't get anything cheaper than Staffordshire and
what about my business?"

"Sell that too, start again elsewhere."

"You're being very negative, Sue. It just can't be done."

"Can you really blame me? Sure it can be done. People
up sticks all the time. I want us to go somewhere
completely different, completely away from the
memories. Otherwise, I can't really see there being an
'us' anymore."

"You don't mean that, Sue."

"I do….." Sue was contemplative and finally said, "Tell
you what - let's go to France. There are cheap places
there. We both have a smattering of French, and we can
take lessons, and the girls will pick it up easily as they are
so young, and our baby……. Oh, don't give up on our
family, Dave."

Dave brooded over the idea for a while, all the pros and
cons, but the idea of the family being broken up, of losing

THE ROUGH CLOSE MURDER

Sue's love won over the cons and he finally said, "Ok, if your mind is made up. I'll look into it."

CONCLUSION

There is a certain contradiction in evidence from witnesses in this murder case, especially as to the number of bullets actually fired, but I have set out the statements as printed in the newspapers.

John Daniel was imprisoned for 20 years at Portland Convict Establishment, Grove, Portland, Dorset. He was released on 13 May, 1901, after serving 15 years. He died on 19 March 1927.

Thomas Daniel, died the year after John's conviction, in 1887 and the house was sold. It was taken over by a Charles Bedson and his second wife Hannah, Charles Bedson being the paternal great grandfather of Heather Poultney, who inspired me to write this book.

Susan Daniel had a baby boy, Thomas Edward, born 1 March 1886. In 1891 the census states she was living at St John the Baptist, Chorlton on Medlock, Lancashire. I can find nothing about this church or if she was actually living in the church or the area. Was she being looked after by the church? In 1901, on his release, John joined his wife and they went to live at 36 Duke Street, Rushholme, in South Manchester.

Their son, Thomas Edward, married Mary Elizabeth Griffin in 1913 at Hulme St. Mary, Manchester. In 1939

154

they were living in Lancashire and he died in Chester in 1956. As for his mother, Susan Daniel, she ended up at Sefton General Hospital, which at the time was Toxteth Park Workhouse, Smithdown Road, in Liverpool. So, Susan Daniel ended up in a workhouse or workhouse infirmary, where she died on 17 February 1927 – a month before her husband, John Daniel.

The workhouse infirmary had been used as a cholera hospital from 1864. Extensive fever wards were built and schooling for boys and girls. By 1893 a large pavilion-style hospital had been erected and, by 1905, a further large hospital complex on the north of the site. Mental wards were erected at the south of the site by 1927. – the same year Susan died. The workhouse later became Smithdown Road Institution and then Sefton General Hospital in 2001. A major clearance of the site took place, in 2001, to make way for a supermarket. A small hospital block at the south-west of the site was then the only surviving workhouse structure.

Dale House farm is no longer a three story house. The top storey was taken off some time in the 1970s.

ACKNOWLEDGEMENTS

Exorcist's Manual by Tarona Hawkins

The Staffordshire Sentinel, Daily and Weekly (Stoke-on-Trent), Mon Mar 1, 1886, Tue Mar 2, 1886, Sat Mar 6 1886 and Sat Mar 13, 1886

The Newcastle Guardian and Silverdale, Chesterton and Audley Chronicle, Newcastle-under-Lyme, Sat Mar 6, 1886

The Tamworth Herald, Sat Mar 6, 1886

Julie Angel, International Psychic Medium

THE ROUGH CLOSE MURDER

https://www.julieangelInternationalpsychicmedium.com

Julie Angel is an International Psychic Medium with over twenty one years' experience. A real life psychic detective, Julie used her abilities whilst in the police service to prevent and detect crime, find missing persons and save three people's lives. She is still regularly called upon today to find missing people, pets and objects!

Her clients include top musicians, sports personalities, actors, actresses as well as TV and radio presenters. Her passion though is helping people from all walks of life whether it is connecting them to people they have loved and lost or shedding some insight on how their life is unfolding. Her national and global predictions can be found on her new page on this her website "Global predictions".

GHOST BUSTING AND EXORCISMS!

Julie is able to remove negative entities from people, their homes and places of employment. "I used to call this side of my work 'house clearances' but people thought I was in the furniture removal trade!

Ghosts haunt for numerous reasons and unfortunately are far too much of an in-depth discussion to detail here. What I can say is that I am discreet, sympathetic and very professional in my work and so far, the hauntings that I have removed have never returned. Ghost busting can be potentially dangerous but due to my approach and psychic protection I have not experienced any major problems, and I must say that I hope it stays that way!
....

Julie is available for 1-2-1 readings, public demonstrations, corporate/hospitality nights, parties, paranormal investigations, ghost busting and exorcisms, psychic and spiritual development classes, and spiritual church services. She is an avid charity fundraiser and is available for evenings of clairvoyance and 'Street Psychic Events" to raise money and awareness for good causes.

She has been head hunted for television, radio and articles in women's magazines including Red, Woman's Own and Take a Break Fate and Fortune. She has also been in The Sun, News of the World, the Sunday People,

Action Wales magazine as well as local press. She has worked for Barcelo Hotels, Costa Coffee, Greene King, Olde English Inns, Moto Services, Chef and Brewer amongst other leading chains. She has been used for ghost hunts at high profile venues such as Warwick Castle, Woodchester Mansion, Bodmin Gaol, Clitheroe Castle, Oxford Castle (with Witney television), Pendle Hill, The Ancient Ram Inn amongst other locations.

She is an avid charity fundraiser and is available for evenings of clairvoyance and 'Street Psychic Events" to raise money and awareness for good causes.

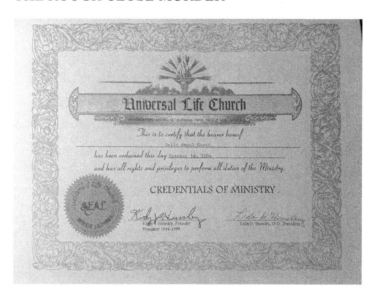

CONTACT:
Please call me on:
Ring or text: 07751 383480
You can find me on Facebook: Julie Angel International
Psychic Medium PAGE.

You can find me on WhatsApp: Julie Angel Psychic
Medium
Instagram Psychicmediumjulieangel
 Or email
julieangelinternationalpsychic@gmail.com
Love and light Julie Angel xxx
 Other historical novels by the author:

Series:

Footsteps in the Past- ISBN 978-0-244-25919-8 This is history turned into a gripping novel. All historical facts are true.

Jane finds herself whisked back in time to 1842, after seeing a ghostly figure running away from the Ash Hall nursing home where she works.

She finds herself working for Job Meigh, the entrepreneur pottery master who built Ash Hall. He was a violent Victorian, but a great philanthropist and a magistrate. He, and industrialist pottery and mine owners had grown rich from the labours of their workers, who were driven to starvation when their pay was repeatedly cut. The Chartists wanted to get the People's Charter approved by Parliament to offer the people representation in Parliament and the vote. This was rejected, resulting in the violent Pottery Riots.

Jane has to discover why she has been sent back into the past and how to get back, and gets involved with the riots – which lead her into life- threatening danger. She also has to find out who the ghostly figure was.

5* Review
"It is an enchanting story, which became more gripping as you read on. It is an historical fantasy set in Ash Hall which, in the past, was the palatial residence of Job Meigh (now a nursing home). Some years ago I visited Ash Hall as my family were looking for somewhere where my mother could be cared for, as she had suffered a devastating stroke. The building oozed history and atmosphere, which comes out clearly in the book. I enjoyed it very much, mainly because the locations were familiar to me, as I had lived in the area all my life. I don't usually read novels, so this one has been the exception."

5* Review
"I have enjoyed reading this book. The history of Ash Hall plus the struggle the working class had to go through to achieve changes to the law."

THE ROUGH CLOSE MURDER

Footsteps in the Past – The Secret –

ISBN 978-0-355-63374-2 The Secret takes the main characters 39 years on from the Pottery Riots of 1842. There is a mining disaster in Bucknall, Stoke, in which Jane and John's son is involved. While nursing John back to health, after his attempt to rescue their son, Jane reminisces what has happened since they met.

Her stories unravel while desperately awaiting news if their son is still alive or not. All historical facts are true.

5* review:

"I bought this book for a Mother's Day present for my mother-in-law. She thoroughly enjoyed reading it. It bought back lots of memories for her. I would recommend the book. Well done, Margaret."

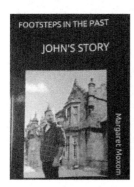

Footsteps in the Past – John's Story –

ISBN 978-1-716-16818-127
This tells John's story from his youth in the countryside village of Hanley in the 1820s through its industrialisation. It tells John's poignant story of his life, loves and losses in the background of the traumatic times and struggles of people fighting for their rights, representation in Parliament and the vote, which lead to the Pottery Riots of 1842. It also tells of the Cholera Pandemic of 1832 similar to Covid today) and his time in the workhouse.

5* review:
"The author has very cleverly brought together local history of the period, using the local dialect of the Potteries, and also weaving a story through it.

The story draws the reader into the times of the Chartists' riots and, while reading this book, I got a real sense of the hard lives of the characters and how frightening it must have been at this time for people having to fight for a living wage. I felt that I knew these people as their story unfolded. The author must have done an awesome amount of research on, not only the history, but the dialect too."

Munford-Gunn – ISBN 97985-322-313-68 This is a dramatic and thrilling true adventure story following two families of pioneers trying to get to Utah, America to escape prejudice for their beliefs. They meet other prejudice along the way, this time against Africans and First Nation Indians. The book is based on true-life reports.

The families make the life-threatening journey by sailing ship (taking six weeks in those days to cross the Atlantic) then join ox-drawn wagon trains, walking beside these across the 1,300 miles of searing hot plains, dragging the wagons through rivers and perilously hauling them up and over the mountains to get to Salt Lake City. Many die along the way of starvation, dehydration and disease.

The two families meet up. Ann Munford marries George Gunn, only to have to set out immediately to clear land and build settlements – that is until the Black Hawk Wars start.

5* Review: "What a nightmare. I had to keep reminding myself to breathe. Going to make a cup of tea to get over the trauma. The description is brilliant. I felt I was right there with them."

THE ROUGH CLOSE MURDER

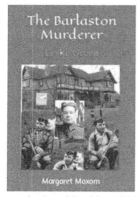

The Barlaston Murderer – Leslie Green
ISBN 979875449770

This is the story of the brutal murder of Mrs Mary Maud Wiltshaw, n 16th July 1952, at her home – going by the name of 'Estoril' on Station Road, Barlaston, Stoke-on-Trent.

Leslie Green, former chauffeur of the Wiltshaws, was hanged for the murder on 23rd December 1952, but right up to the moment of the noose going around his neck, he denied carrying out the murder, saying he was elsewhere – asleep on a park bench. I was intrigued by this – did he do the murder or not? Yes, you can say that he was a loser, a thief, and that drink played a part in the attack – possibly. I was also intrigued by the fact that he presented himself to the police station of his own accord. Now, why would he do that, if he had committed the murder? Also, there was a later deathbed confession that was not investigated.

This book sets out the actual police investigations and trial that led to his sentence of hanging, taken from newspapers at the time. However, I wanted to give another possible side of the story, that could conceivably have had a bearing on Leslie Green's state of mind at the time – a mind that, from his early childhood and mistreatment, had manifested itself into loss of memory – when he experienced a sense of 'loss of time' - when another personality took over.

Please note that this is a completely fictitious notion but seemed to fit the bill. None of the history of Leslie Green before the trial, apart from his prosecutions, is factual or could be verified, despite meticulous investigations.

5* Review:
"A fascinating insight into a vicious crime.

The Barlaston murder is a subject I have been aware of for many years, but this book has really brought me up to date. The main character – Leslie Green – has left little in the form of an historical footprint. This is possibly due to his being hung shortly after the trial. I don't think there should be any apology for his story being filled in by way of a fictional account of him. This makes for a thought-provoking process which calls into question the legal system of the 1950s, whilst retaining respect for the victim."

THE ROUGH CLOSE MURDER

Printed in Great Britain
by Amazon

24637041R00096